THE SEASONAL VARIATION
OF INTEREST RATES

The Seasonal Variation

of Interest Rates

STANLEY DILLER

Occasional Paper 108

National Bureau of Economic Research
New York 1969
Distributed by Columbia University Press
New York and London

 1

106428

RELATION OF THE DIRECTORS TO THE WORK AND PUBLICATIONS OF THE NATIONAL BUREAU OF ECONOMIC RESEARCH

1. The object of the National Bureau of Economic Research is to ascertain and to present to the public important economic facts and their interpretation in a scientific and impartial manner. The Board of Directors is charged with the responsibility of ensuring that the work of the National Bureau is carried on in strict conformity with this object.

2. The President of the National Bureau shall submit to the Board of Directors, or to its Executive Committee, for their formal adoption all specific proposals for research to be instituted.

3. No research report shall be published until the President shall have submitted to each member of the Board the manuscript proposed for publication, and such information as will, in his opinion and in the opinion of the author, serve to determine the suitability of the report for publication in accordance with the principles of the National Bureau. Each manuscript shall contain a summary drawing attention to the nature and treatment of the problem studied, the character of the data and their utilization in the report, and the main conclusions reached.

4. For each manuscript so submitted, a special committee of the Board shall be appointed by majority agreement of the President and Vice Presidents (or by the Executive Committee in case of inability to decide on the part of the President and Vice Presidents), consisting of three directors selected as nearly as may be one from each general division of the Board. The names of the special manuscript committee shall be stated to each Director when the manuscript is submitted to him. It shall be the duty of each member of the special manuscript committee to read the manuscript. If each member of the manuscript committee signifies his approval within thirty days of the transmittal of the manuscript, the report may be published. If at the end of that period any member of the manuscript committee withholds his approval, the President shall then notify each member of the Board, requesting approval or disapproval of publication, and thirty days additional shall be granted for this purpose. The manuscript shall then not be published unless at least a majority of the entire Board who shall have voted on the proposal within the time fixed for the receipt of votes shall have approved.

5. No manuscript may be published, though approved by each member of the special manuscript committee, until forty-five days have elapsed from the transmittal of the report in manuscript form. The interval is allowed for the receipt of any memorandum of dissent or reservation, together with a brief statement of his reasons, that any member may wish to express; and such memorandum of dissent or reservation shall be published with the manuscript if he so desires. Publication does not, however, imply that each member of the Board has read the manuscript, or that either members of the Board in general or the special committee have passed on its validity in every detail.

6. Publications of the National Bureau issued for informational purposes concerning the work of the Bureau and its staff, or issued to inform the public of activities of Bureau staff, and volumes issued as a result of various conferences involving the National Bureau shall contain a specific disclaimer noting that such publication has not passed through the normal review procedures required in this resolution. The Executive Committee of the Board is charged with review of all such publications from time to time to ensure that they do not take on the character of formal research reports of the National Bureau, requiring formal Board approval.

7. Unless otherwise determined by the Board or exempted by the terms of paragraph 6, a copy of this resolution shall be printed in each National Bureau publication.

(Resolution adopted October 25, 1926, and revised February 6, 1933,
February 24, 1941, and April 20, 1968)

CONTENTS

TABLES

CHARTS

ACKNOWLEDGEMENTS

The late William H. Brown, Jr., left a partial manuscript on the present subject that contributed to this study. In addition I discussed various aspects of the study with Geoffrey Moore, Phillip Cagan, Jack Guttentag, Anna Schwartz, Otto Eckstein, Walter D. Fisher and Walter E. Hoadley, all of whom read at least one draft of the paper. Although I acted on many of their comments, I assume full responsibility for the results.

Jae Won Lee assisted me from the beginning both in the considerable data handling involved, as well as in the development of the ideas.

H. Irving Forman drew the charts, and Gnomi Schrift Gouldin both edited the manuscript and handled the production arrangements.

STANLEY DILLER

CHAPTER 1

Introduction

ALTHOUGH VARIATIONS in interest rates coinciding with the seasons of the year were virtually nonexistent during the 1930's and World War II, they reappeared in the late 1940's and grew in amplitude during the 1950's. The amplitude reached a high point between 1957 and 1959 then diminished substantially in the early 1960's. These gyrations have attracted wide attention among money market analysts. The seasonal movement in short-term rates reached a peak in December and a trough in July. It constituted 20 per cent of the average level of the interest rates. For long-term rates the movement was considerably less. In the past year or so the seasonal has shown new vigor.

A study of the seasonal variation of interest rates contributes to our understanding of the money market and the behavior of interest rates. Interest rates depend upon the supply and demand for credit; therefore, the seasonal variation of credit conditions is likely to contain an explanation of seasonal movements in rates. There is a well known and long standing increase in the economy's demand for short-term credit in the fall and early winter and a corresponding decrease in the late spring and summer. There is an equally well known increase in the supply of Federal Reserve credit in the fall and early winter and a withdrawal of credit in the late spring and summer. The sea-

1

sonal in short-term rates depends upon a combination of the seasonals in the demand and supply for credit. In years of unusually high demand for credit in the fall combined with a smaller increase in supply (and vice versa for late spring and early summer), the seasonal in interest rates will be large. When the seasonal changes in supply and demand are offsetting, no seasonal appears in interest rates. The amount of change in supply required to offset a change in demand is a statistical question considered in Chapter 4.

The determination and measurement of seasonal movements are hindered by other sources of variation in economic factors, as well as by the volatility of the seasonal component itself. While statistical methods differ in detail, they all attempt to isolate the seasonal component from the other sources of variation and to determine its size and stability. Chapter 2 of this study describes some of the methods used to measure seasonal movements, and Chapter 3 considers in some detail the application of one of these methods to a variety of interest rate series.

The method used here is that currently used by the U.S. Bureau of the Census. The nonseasonal variation of the series is captured by a long-term moving average designed to eliminate any seasonal movements. Each term in the time series is then separated into a moving average component and a component consisting of the difference or ratio of the original series to the moving average. If a series has no seasonal component, the ratios will tend to average unity (the differences, zero) for each set of observations relating to a specific month; that is, the mean of all the ratios calculated for July or November (or any other month) will tend to equal unity, and all such means will of necessity tend to be equal. There will, of course, be observable differences in the mean ratios because of erratic movements in the series, but none of these differences will be significantly different from unity. Thus, averages that do differ significantly from unity provide evidence of seasonality.

The remainder of this chapter describes and analyzes the pattern of seasonal variations in interest rates over the 1948–65 period and discusses some historical developments which are widely thought to have influenced these patterns.

SHORT-TERM RATES

Short-term rates typically decline from a relative high in January through seasonally neutral February, to a trough in June or July, then sharply incline past seasonally neutral August to September, gradually rising to a peak in December. Chart 1 plots the seasonal factors for 1951, 1957, and 1965 (the years before, during and after the period of peak seasonality) for the four short-term rates studied, and Chart 2 shows the factors for call-money rates in 1915 computed by Macaulay.[1]

Seasonal variation of interest rates is the net result of seasonal variation in both the supply and demand for credit, arising when the effect of a given variable on demand is not offset by a comparable movement in supply, as in the following description of an earlier period:

Before the establishment of the Federal Reserve System, there were four more or less distinct seasonal variations in interest rates. . . . The first movement, from early January until about the middle of February, is characterized by low interest rates, . . . attributable to the fact that the crop movement, with its great demand for money in the West and South, has passed its peak, and has been followed by a heavy flow of cash from the country banks to the primary money market. At the same time, the demand for funds is relatively slack, for business in general is characteristically full during the interval between the holidays and the opening of the spring manufacturing and trading season.

The second period, which is marked by rising interest rates, is largely attributable to the monetary demand of producers and manufacturers. This demand is supplemented, particularly in the latter part of the period, by crop planting requirements.

The third important seasonal variation is that of a weakening money market in April and May, followed by a genuine depression in June and July. This period at its beginning reflects a declining demand for funds by the manufacturing and producing interests of the industrial centers,

[1] The 1915 factors are given in Frederick R. Macaulay, *Some Theoretical Problems Suggested by the Movements of Interest Rates, Bond Yields and Stock Prices in the United States since 1856*, New York, NBER, 1938, insert after p. 216. The method used to compute the recent factors is described briefly in Chapter 2. Here it suffices to note that a factor exceeding 100.0 implies a seasonal high. The factors for the postwar period were computed with the Census Bureau's X-11 seasonal adjustment program.

CHART 1

Seasonal Factors on Short-Term Securities for Selected Years

1. Treasury bills
2. Commercial paper
3. Bankers acceptances
4. U. S. government securities, 9 to 12 months

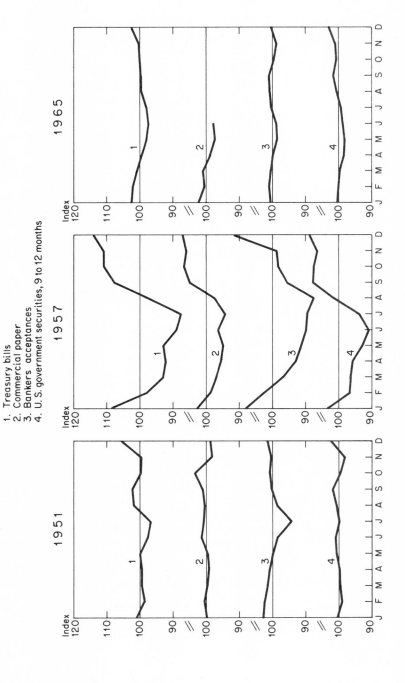

CHART 2

Seasonal Factors for Yield on Call Money,
Macaulay's Series, 1915

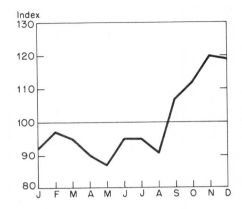

and in its latter stages the return of funds from the country districts following the completion of the crop planting period.

The fourth season is generally referred to as the crop moving period. The demand for funds in the country districts for the paying of farm labor, the storing of grain, and the moving of produce to the primary markets calls for an outflow of funds from the financial centers to the interior. At the same time, the demand from producing and manufacturing enterprises which are making ready for the fall trade becomes very heavy, thus bringing added pressure to bear on the financial markets. This period ordinarily reaches a peak in October, with interest rates commonly remaining high till January.[2]

What, then, are the present sources of seasonal influence on the demand for credit? These sources are likely to be found in wholesale and retail trade; government fiscal activity, particularly short-term borrowing in autumn to close the gap between tax revenues and expenditures; corporate demand for credit to finance tax and dividend payments in the final quarter of the year, which may be regarded as an increased demand for credit or as a diminished supply of funds that at other times are available to finance government and trade debt; and no doubt other factors as well.[3]

[2] Richard N. Owens and Charles O. Hardy, *Interest Rates and Stock Speculation,* Washington, D.C., The Brookings Institution, 1930, pp. 3–5.

[3] One measure of the diminished supply of corporate investment funds in autumn is the increase in government dealer positions, although other forces

During the fifty years preceding the adoption of the Federal Reserve Act in 1914, seasonal changes in the demand for currency confronted a virtually inelastic currency supply. This situation caused steep movements in both short-term interest rates and, with the fractional reserve system, in the money supply itself. One of the Federal Reserve System's initial objectives was to facilitate the easy transfer of deposits into currency, thereby preventing the sudden declines in the supply of money that had attended the seasonal increases in the demand for currency. Their success in this regard is conspicuous in the contrast between the seasonal amplitudes both in currency outstanding and in short-term interest rates during the periods before and after 1914. The seasonal amplitude of currency outstanding increased substantially in the later period because of the more elastic supply, as well as, given the smaller amplitudes of short-term interest rates, the reduced incentive to economize on its use.[4]

Federal Reserve activity, however, did not entirely eliminate the seasonal variation in short-term interest rates. Seasonal influences persisted, although with much smaller amplitude, throughout the 1920's. In the 1930's, with bank reserves well above legal requirements, seasonal variation in short-term interest rates was barely perceptible despite the absence of the Federal Reserve's seasonal influence. Again in the 1940's, with interest rates pegged within narrow limits, there was little room for seasonal variation. It was only when the authorities removed the peg—gradually in the 1951–53 period—that seasonal variation in short-term rates reappeared. Erratic at first, and with a small amplitude, the seasonal pattern became more systematic in the late 1950's, when its amplitude exceeded 10 per cent on either side of the level of rates. After 1959, however, the seasonal amplitude quickly collapsed and became a mere ripple by

affect these positions as well. Dealer holdings of government securities increase, on average, by 33 per cent in December when compared with the preceding June, one study found. See U.S. Congress, Joint Economic Committee, *A Study of the Dealer Market For Federal Securities,* Washington, D.C., 1960, p. 41.

[4] The change in the seasonal amplitude of call money rates is shown graphically in Macaulay, *op. cit.,* p. 217. The change in the seasonal amplitudes of currency outstanding is described in Milton Friedman and Anna Schwartz, *A Monetary History of the United States, 1867–1960,* Princeton for NBER, 1963, p. 293. The smaller the autumn increase in rates the less is the need to rely on money substitutes, such as trade credit, or to increase the velocity of currency.

1963.[5] The seasonal variation in the period following the Treasury-Federal Reserve accord of 1951 is alike, both in its evolution over the period and its pattern, for the four short-term rates studied: commercial paper, bankers' acceptances, nine- to twelve-month Treasury securities, and 91-day Treasury bills. The variation is similar, moreover, to the pattern Macaulay found for call-money rates during the early part of the century; a surprising similarity, in view of the changes in the capital markets resulting from the relatively recent prominence of government fiscal activity.

This study has not attempted a systematic analysis of the factors affecting seasonal variation in the demand for credit. It may be merely coincidental that the changes over time in the incidence and importance of the factors affecting the seasonal variation of demand have not substantially altered the seasonal pattern of interest rates. The timing of crop movements in the earlier period appears to have affected the seasonal demand for credit in approximately the same pattern as the more important fiscal influences do today. There has been, however, some variation in the timing of fiscal activity that appears to have affected the seasonal variation of interest rates. (This variation is considered in Chapter 4.) Apart from this variation the significant difference between the early and later periods lies not in the variation of demand factors but rather in the conditions of supply. Whereas in the pre-Federal Reserve period the means of accommodating the supply to changes in the demand for credit were limited, these means were virtually unlimited in the later period. Since interest rates vary in response to differences in the rates of

---

[5] The evidence for these statements is presented in Chapter 3.

While this study was in final manuscript form seasonal adjustments through the middle of 1968 became available. These data reveal an apparent resurgence of seasonal variation in both short- and long-term rates. Whereas this study calculated a seasonal factor for Treasury bills in December 1965 of 102.6, the more recent data indicate a factor of 104.6 for December 1967. In the case of long-term U.S. government bonds the figures for September, the peak month for this series, are 100.3 and 101.0 for 1965 and 1967, respectively. By the nature of the adjustment process inclusion of the more recent data will alter the calculated factors for earlier years. The factors for the last three years reported in this study are therefore subject to upward revision just as the most recent figures would be if the seasonal were to change subsequently. (Seasonal factors are measures of seasonal change. The method of computing them is described in Chapter 2.)

change of supply and demand, the ability to vary the supply implies the ability to remove the seasonal factor in interest rates. Of course, the ability to offset changes in demand requires recognition of those changes, the failure of which would result in an unwanted seasonal influence on interest rates.

That the Federal Reserve did not exercise its ability to expunge the seasonal variation in interest rates does not *imply* an error in judgment. It is arguable, in fact, whether the Federal Reserve should eliminate the seasonality in interest rates—an argument that rests largely on whether removing the symptom of monetary tightness would tend to aggravate the cause of the problem. Just as palliating a sore throat with syrup to increase one's temporary tolerance for cigarettes at the expense of subsequent aggravation, the attempt to ease the cyclical tightness in the money market with infusions of money will stimulate inflationary forces. It is doubtful, however, that a similar response to the more ephemeral seasonal tightness would provoke excessive demand for productive resources—especially in view of the contraction of the money supply some months later that a seasonal monetary policy implies.[6]

In a later chapter this paper argues that the seasonal pattern, if any, of interest rates is determined by the factors affecting the demand for credit; while the seasonal amplitude is determined by the degree of accommodation of the supply of credit.

LONG-TERM RATES [7]

While few would contest the occurrence of seasonal shifts in the demand for money or the possibility that the Federal Reserve allows

[6] For a discussion of whether the Federal Reserve should accommodate short-period fluctuations in the demand for credit see Jack Guttentag, "The Strategy of Open Market Operations," *Quarterly Journal of Economics,* February, 1966, 23–25, and the references cited there.

[7] The computation of the monthly bond yields used in this study is described in the *Federal Reserve Bulletin* as follows:

U.S. Govt. bonds: Averages of daily figures for bonds maturing or callable in 10 years or more. *State and local govt. bonds:* General obligations only, based on Thurs. figures. *Corporate bonds:* Averages of daily figures.

"Corporate" bonds comprise industrials, rails, and utilities. Remarks made about monthly movements do not reflect intramonth variation. Evaluation of this variation requires use of weekly or sometimes daily figures, which is beyond the scope of this study.

these shifts to affect short-term interest rates, seasonal variation in long-term rates is another matter. There are no obvious reasons for seasonality in long-term rates and some cogent reasons for its absence. To meet seasonal needs for cash corporations, including banks, seldom sell off long-term securities and thereby raise rates. Firms, moreover, can usually delay their long-term borrowing to take advantage of seasonal (i.e., expected) declines in rates; and in so doing eliminate the seasonal variations. Finally, seasonality of sufficient amplitude would invite arbitrage; that is, investors would buy bonds when rates were high and sell them, say, six months later when rates fell—reducing their incentive in the process. To invite arbitrage the seasonal amplitude must be large enough to cover the significant transaction costs involved in holding long-term securities for limited periods. Rough calculations with respect to the orders of magnitude involved may be found in Chapter 4.[8]

This study has found significant seasonal movement in all of the long-term securities examined. The evolution of the seasonal pattern over the postwar period resembles that for short-term rates, with a peak in the late fifties, and the pattern, similar for each of the long-term securities, leads that for short-term rates by about three months. Chart 3 compares the 1958 seasonal factor for bankers' acceptances and municipal bonds (highest rating). The seasonal amplitude of long-term rates is much smaller than that of short-term rates, seldom exceeding 3 per cent on either side of the average level during the period of peak seasonality in the late fifties. The common evolution of the longs and shorts together with the inverse relation between seasonal amplitude and term to maturity is shown in Chart 4. This chart, restricted to government securities—ninety-day, nine- to twelve-month, three- to five-year, and long-term Treasury securities—plots the variances, computed separately for each year and each security, of

[8] Some additional constraints allow the short-term markets fewer opportunities for arbitrage. Since there is usually six months between the seasonal peak and trough, both for the long- and short-term securities, it is not possible to hold, say, 91-day Treasury bills over the full range of variation—that is, from peak to trough or the reverse. Moreover, while yields on long-term securities differ imperceptibly between, say, a nineteen and one-half and a twenty year maturity, the yield curve for short-term securities has a substantial slope. Therefore, the typically higher yield on six-month compared with three-month securities may nullify the advantage of borrowing for six months at low summer rates instead of for three months at high winter rates. Chapter 4 considers this point in greater detail.

CHART 3

Seasonal Factors for Bankers' Acceptance Rates and Yields
on Municipal Bonds, Highest Rating, 1958

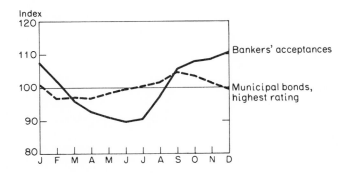

the twelve monthly seasonal factors. Since the variance measures the dispersion of the factors around 100.0, it is a good summary statistic for the seasonal amplitude.[9] These bell-shaped curves neatly sketch the rise and fall in the amplitude of the seasonal components of the four series and order them with respect to seasonal amplitude. The symmetry of the four curves after 1952 is as remarkable as their movements before 1952 are inscrutable. The seasonal amplitude of each of the four series rises steadily from 1952 to its peak in 1957 and then falls off at approximately the same rate at which it rose. After 1952, the evolution of the seasonal factors is virtually identical in all four sets of securities.

This statement, of course, implies nothing about the reliability of the estimates of the seasonal factors, the determination of which is the main objective of this study. Chapter 3 concludes, for example, that long-term government bonds evinced no significant seasonality outside the period 1955–60; whereas it finds a significant though small seasonal pattern in the private long-term bonds throughout most of the postwar period. These issues will be considered in greater detail in Chapter 3.

For most of the long-term series considered, 1955 divides the postwar period into two parts with distinctly different seasonal patterns. Typically, the earlier pattern starts with a January low and falls

[9] To conserve space the curves are plotted on four-cycle semi-log paper.

slightly to a trough in March, then rises through May (roughly 100.0) to a plateau extending from June through October, and afterwards returns to the 100.0 level for November and December. Although the general patterns for all the private long-term bonds agree with this picture, there are differences in detail. For most series the plateau

CHART 4

Variances of Seasonal Factors of Yields on U.S. Government Securities, 1948–65

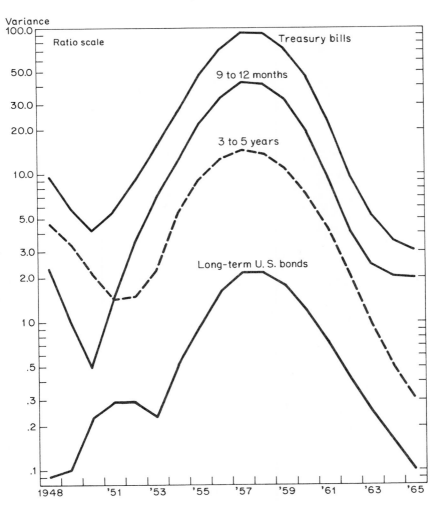

actually tilts toward a peak, usually in September but sometimes in June or October. The patterns for all the private long-term bonds are alike with respect to their midyear highs and January lows, the characteristics of which distinguish these patterns from those of the same securities in the later period, as well as from the patterns of the short-term rates. Chart 5 plots the seasonal factors for 1954 for selected private long-term rates.

Starting in 1955, the seasonal patterns of private long-term bond rates change. The January factors change from lows to highs, the June and July factors from highs to lows. The troughs remain in March and April and the peaks in September and October, the amplitude on these months increasing during the late fifties and tapering off afterward.

Chart 6 illustrates the differences in both pattern and amplitudes between the two periods for two long-term rates. Starting roughly at

CHART 5

Seasonal Factors for Yields on Selected Long-Term
Securities, 1954

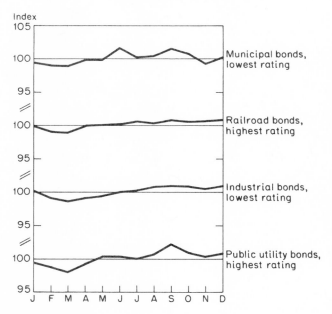

CHART 6

Seasonal Factors for Yields on Corporate Bonds and
Industrial Bonds, Highest Rating, 1952 and 1957

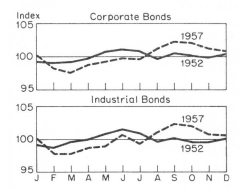

the 100.0 line in January, the 1957 factor curve drops to a trough in March and gradually rises, crossing the 100.0 line in July to a peak in September, from which it declines to the December position, slightly above the 100.0 line. Unlike the Treasury securities, this pattern persists, though with diminished amplitude, at least through 1963 and, for some series, all the way to 1965.

Unfortunately, analysis of seasonality is not founded on principles that permit the unambiguous determination that a seasonal influence exists at a given time, and whether it is significant or otherwise. Aside from some special cases there are no criteria whose satisfaction provides compelling evidence for or against the existence of seasonality. In many cases, perhaps most cases, this hiatus is academic in the sense that an experienced analyst can profitably rely on his judgment, and forego the statistical accouterments, to test for seasonality, although, even here, the problem remains of making the point-estimates of the seasonal factors for the adjustment itself. In borderline cases, however, when the evidence for seasonality is not conclusive, intuitive methods invite disagreement. The dearth of adjusted data for interest rates in the postwar period combined with the widely held belief that a seasonal pattern did exist at least for some of the rates over part of the period is strong evidence that interest rates are a borderline case. Chapter 2 reviews the concepts underlying seasonal analysis and some of the methods used for adjustment.[10] Chapter 3, then, considers the evidence of seasonality in interest rates. Chapter 4 analyzes factors contributing to the extent of seasonal amplitude of both short- and long-term rates and tests a hypothesis relating the seasonal amplitude of short-term rates to that of the money supply. Chapter 5 summarizes the report and lists some conclusions.

[10] Those readers already familiar with seasonal analysis can skip this chapter without loss of continuity.

CHAPTER 2

---◆▶---

Methods of Seasonal Adjustment

INTRODUCTION

IT IS OFTEN USEFUL to separate a time series into components that differ in the frequency of their recurrence. Some series, national income, for example, tend to increase over time, to have a positive trend—although any given observation may be smaller than its predecessor because it happens to fall on the down side of a different component, whether cyclical, seasonal, irregular, or some anonymous component. Since each observation is assumed to be the result of the separate influences of each component, to capture the effect on the series of any given component requires that the others be in some way filtered out. Perhaps the main reason for using seasonally adjusted data is to facilitate identification of the cyclical component.[1]

It is sometimes profitable to study the behavior of a particular component for what it reveals about the behavior of the composite series. Investment and interest rates, for example, are sometimes observed to vary together over the course of the business cycle because shifts in the demand for investment goods dwarf the movements along the curve. By abstracting from the cyclical component of either

---

[1] See Julius Shiskin and Harry Eisenpress, *Seasonal Adjustment by Electronic Computer Methods,* Technical Paper No. 12, NBER, 1958. Represented in *Business Cycle Indicators,* Volume 1, Princeton for NBER, 1961.

series it may be possible to observe the expected inverse relation, at a given time, between the two series. Ultimately, since the several components of a series are distinct only because they are determined by different factors (by different variables or by different patterns of variation of the same variables), the identification of the components is a step toward the goal of explaining their behavior.[2] In practice, because of the difficulty of specifying those models describing the behavior of each component, the two goals are distinguished and, ordinarily, the second one eschewed.

One way to eliminate from the variation of the combined series that part due to one of the components is to smooth the series with a moving average of which the number of terms equals the period of the recurring variation of that component. Consider, for example, a daily series of retail sales: Every Sunday there is a sharp drop. By replacing each daily value of the series with the value of a centered seven-term moving average—in other words, by replacing, say, the original Wednesday value with the average of the preceding three days, that Wednesday, and the following three days, and similarly for the other days—one obtains a series that is free of the recurring variation. When the moving average is subtracted from or divided into the original series, a new series emerges containing samples of all the components for which the variation has a period of seven or less.

Since seasonal variation is defined as variation that recurs in a period not greater than a year, there is no need to distinguish, for the purpose of seasonal adjustment, among components whose variation recurs in periods exceeding one year. It is enough to smooth the seasonal variation with a twelve-term moving average (assuming monthly data) and use the deviations of the composite series from the moving average as estimates of the components, the period of whose recurring variation does not exceed one year. The moving average is then an estimate of the trend-cycle or low frequency component of the series, and the deviations from it of the seasonal and irregular components. These deviations, usually expressed as ratios of the composite series to the trend-cycle component, are the

[2] Horst Mendershausen, "Annual Survey of Statistical Technique: Methods of Computing and Eliminating Changing Seasonal Fluctuations," *Econometrica,* 1937, pp. 234–62.

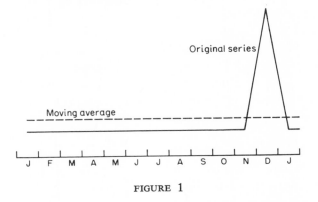

Original series

Moving average

J F M A M J J A S O N D J

FIGURE 1

raw data for the seasonal adjustment. They are called the seasonal-irregular (SI) ratios.[3]

SEASONAL-IRREGULAR RATIOS

The SI ratios, expressed as percentages, are computed for each month of each year. The twelve SI ratios for each year are adjusted to force their sum to 1200. This adjustment precludes any discrepancy between the *expected values* of the totals for any consecutive twelve months (as distinct from the observed totals for a given year) [4] of the seasonally adjusted series and the totals of the original series. Year to year changes of the series are therefore unaffected, on average,

[3] When the deviations are expressed as ratios, the adjustment is called multiplicative; when expressed as differences, additive. In the Census Bureau's X-11 seasonal adjustment program, as well as in earlier versions of the program, computation of the SI ratios is a much more complicated procedure than the one described above. First a thirteen-term moving average is computed (half weights at the end points) and divided into the original data. The preliminary SI ratios are adjusted for extreme values and smoothed into moving seasonal factors (to be described below). The preliminary factors are divided into the original series to get a preliminarily adjusted series. A Henderson curve, an elastic moving average of varying terms, is fitted to the adjusted series, and a new set of SI ratios computed, adjusted for extremes and smoothed into a moving average into the final seasonal factors. See Shiskin and Eisenpress, *op. cit.*, and the *X-11 Variant of the Census Method II Seasonal Adjustment Program*, Washington, D.C., U.S. Department of Commerce, Bureau of the Census, Technical Paper No. 15, 1965 (hereafter referred to as the X-11 manual).

[4] Arthur Burns and Wesley C. Mitchell, *Measuring Business Cycles*, New York, NBER, 1946, p. 51.

by seasonal adjustment, while the variation within years is redistributed to eliminate the effect of systematic intrayear variation.

The symmetry thus imposed on the SI ratios reveals an important property of seasonal adjustment; the interrelatedness of the seasonal factors among several months. Consider a series in which the values for the first eleven months of the year are equal (they could even be zero) but for the twelfth month very high.[5] Graphically, the series is shown in Figure 1. To maintain the symmetry of the SI ratios the high point in December must be balanced by a low point elsewhere. Since the datum for the highs and lows is the trend cycle curve, in this case a twelve-term moving average, the symmetry is achieved by raising the datum above the values for the first eleven months of the series thereby imputing seasonal lows to these values. Through its influence on the moving average, the December high in effect creates the January-to-November lows.

There is clearly a certain arbitrariness in imputing significance to the deviations from the moving average. The arbitrariness resides in the connotation of normality attached to the moving average from which the deviations appear, therefore, to be atypical and to invite behavioral explanations. Using a crude method for ascertaining the extent of seasonality in the capital markets, a method that did not abstract from the effects of trend, Kemmerer drew the following conclusion:

> The national bank-note circulation curves do not appear to exhibit any considerable seasonal elasticity, i.e., rise and fall according to the seasonal variations in the demands of trade; it is noteworthy, however, that the increase in the circulation, which takes place normally from year to year, takes place largely in the fall and early winter. Apparently banks intending to increase their circulation postpone doing so until the crop-moving season approaches, so that the year's normal increase takes place principally in the latter part of the year. There is no evidence of contraction when the crop-moving demands are over, the national bank-note elasticity being (to use a rather inelegant expression) of the chewing gum variety. Here, however, . . . it is fortunate that the increase which normally does take place each year takes place in the season when it is needed most.[6]

[5] This hypothetical series is chosen only for simplicity. The principle involved, however, does not depend on the simplicity of the sample.

[6] Edwin W. Kemmerer, *Seasonal Variations in the Demands for Currency and Capital,* Washington, D.C., National Monetary Commission, Vol. XXII, 1911, p. 153.

Had the ratio-to-moving average method of seasonal analysis been available at the time of his study, Kemmerer would probably have affirmed the presence of seasonality in the series because of the effect of the high values in the autumn on the trend-cycle values for the rest of the year. Whether a series declines seasonally in a given month depends not on its average value in the month relative to its average value in the previous month—the averages being taken across years—but on the average of its values relative to what they would have been in the absence of seasonality. A series with positive trend is expected to increase from, say, April to May; by remaining constant, on average, it in effect declines relative to the expectation. The arbitrariness resides, therefore, only in the assumed existence of smooth, independent components in fixed relation in the hypothetical population from which the series is drawn.[7]

STABLE SEASONAL FACTORS

Estimated stable seasonal factors are defined as the mean value of the SI ratios for each month. They are called stable or constant because they are computed once for the entire sample period. Any deviation of the SI ratios computed for a given month from the factor computed for that month is attributed to the irregular component. In other words, the SI ratios consist of a systematic and a random component called, respectively, the seasonal and the irregular components. Since the irregular component, expressed as a fraction of the seasonal component, is defined to vary with equal likelihood above and below the seasonal component, its ratio to the seasonal component is on average equal to 1. (In the additive case the mean of the irregular component is zero.) Therefore, the mean SI ratio,

[7] Using a twelve-month average instead of, say, a six-month or eighteen-month average as the datum for seasonality is also arbitrary unless "the activity represented by a series has a 'natural' business year, with a definite beginning and end, as in movements of products from farms. . . . In the absence of a natural year, there is no basis other than convention for selecting the boundaries of the year; . . . the final seasonal adjustment will then vary with the boundaries selected." Burns and Mitchell, *op. cit.,* p. 49 fn. In commenting thus Burns and Mitchell were concerned with a particular method of adjustment, the Kuznets amplitude-ratio method (described later); although the principle is apropos of any method.

say for January, is equal to the seasonal component, assumed to be a constant, multiplied by 1. In the absence of seasonality the mean SI ratios would not differ significantly from each other or from 1.

A simple test for the presence of stable seasonality is therefore to determine the statistical significance of the differences among the computed mean SI ratios for each month. The test is a one-way analysis of variance of the monthly SI ratios, twelve columns of them for the twelve months, and the number of rows equalling the number of annual observations.[8] The F-statistic, computed for N full years, is equal to

$$\frac{N \text{ times variance of monthly means}}{\text{total variance minus } N \text{ times variance of monthly means}}$$

Except for the graphic method of fitting smooth curves to SI ratios of a given month over the years most of the earlier methods and many of those used currently result in estimates of stable seasonal factors. For example, the widely used dummy variable technique, whereby the monthly series X is regressed on twelve dummy variables, eleven of which assume the value 1 when the series is measured in a particular month and zero otherwise, the twelfth dummy variable always assumes the value zero, estimates stable seasonal factors.[9] The computation of stable seasonals is justified when there are good reasons for believing that the parameters are stable in the hypothetical population from which the observed series is drawn. This belief is *not* analogous to the assumed constancy of the parameters in the structural relation of, say, consumption and income. A change in the seasonal parameters (as distinct from the estimated factors) of interest rates does not require that the structural relation between, say, interest rates and money supply, change but only that the seasonal pattern of money supply change. In fact, by assuming the structural relation fixed one can, in principle, estimate it by relating the changes in the seasonal pattern of one series to those in the other.[10] Therefore, the assumption

[8] The X-11 performs the analysis of variance test on the SI ratios after they have been modified to reduce the effect of extreme observations. See X-11 manual, *op. cit.*, p. 5.

[9] Michael C. Lovell, "Seasonal Adjustment of Economic Time Series and Multiple Regression Analysis," *American Statistical Association Journal*, December 1963, p. 993.

[10] The distinction here is between a structural relation between two economic variables, on the one hand, and between an economic variable and time, on the other. Economic models assume constancy in the first case but not the

of fixed seasonal parameters for a given series implies the assumption of fixed structural relations between this series and others, as well as of fixed seasonal patterns in these related series.

MOVING SEASONAL FACTORS

Typically there are changes not so much in the original cause of the seasonal movement but in the economy's adaptation to it. The increased demand for funds in the fall months will result in a seasonal high in interest rates only in the absence of a corresponding increase in the supply of funds. The willingness or ability of the banking system to supply the funds will determine whether the increased demand will result in higher rates. Seasonal increases in the demand, as well as in the supply of funds have varied in the postwar period, and the seasonal increase in interest rates has varied along with it.

Changes in seasonal patterns are difficult to distinguish from irregular movements—the more difficult, the greater is the variance of the irregular component relative to that of the total series. One identifies with greater confidence very small changes in the seasonal variation of money supply, a series with an almost negligible irregular component,[11] than changes in the seasonal variation of the highly irregular Treasury bill rate series. The problem of identifying these changes is analogous to one of identifying the components themselves: The method already described for that is predicated on the assumed smoothness of each of the components within its particular frequency; a method for dealing with changes in the components is to assume these changes themselves evolve along a smooth path. This method involves either fitting by eye a smooth curve to the SI ratios for all the Januaries, another for the Februaries, and so on, instead of a straight line at the means of the ratios for each month as in the stable factors, or computing a moving average, one month at a time, of the SI ratios adjusted for extreme values. If a simple three-term moving average were used, for example, the seasonal factor for

second. The fact that a timing relationship has changed does not imply a change in structural relationship since it may reflect merely the timing change of the variables with which it is structurally related.

[11] The variation of the rate of change of the money supply has, of course, a much larger irregular component.

January 1953 would equal the average of the SI ratios for January 1952, 1953, and 1954. In practice, such a simple moving average would be used only for series whose irregular component, being small, is in little danger of distorting the evolution of the seasonal factors. A weighted five-term moving average was used to compute the moving seasonal factors of the interest rate series. When the assumption of gradually evolving seasonal factors is not apposite, the use of this method will impose a spurious similarity on the estimated factors for adjacent years of a given month. However, by observing graphs of the SI ratios themselves one may judge the appropriateness of the method.

There are several alternative methods of calculating moving seasonal factors. The simplest one merely divides the whole sample period into subperiods and computes stable seasonal factors for each of the subperiods. This method is particularly useful for separating the subperiods with clear evidence of seasonality from those without it. There is some evidence, for example, that yields on long-term Treasury securities manifested seasonality during the late fifties but not before or since. A method based on evolving factors would spread the estimated period of seasonality past its true period, at the same time that it dilutes what seasonality there is. The method is also useful when there is an abrupt change in some institutional factor affecting the seasonal pattern, as, for example, when the Treasury-Federal Reserve accord in 1951 removed the peg on U.S. Government bonds. Another method is to compute a set of stable factors for the whole period and, on the assumption that the true factors for any given year remain in fixed relation, compute factors for each year proportional to the stable factors (that is, with an identical pattern but different amplitude). The proportion used for a given year is the regression coefficient obtained by regressing the SI ratios for that year on the stable factors, one regression for each year.[12] The application of this method to the Treasury bill rates would result in an adjustment not very different, and perhaps a little better, than that obtained with the moving average method. This point is considered in the next chapter. Finally, some writers recommend tying the moving seasonal factors of one series to the variation of related variables.

[12] See Simon Kuznets, *Seasonal Variations in Industry and Trade,* New York, NBER, 1933, p. 324.

This method is, of course, limited by the researcher's ability to specify the appropriate relations.[13]

Sometimes the term *moving seasonal* is applied to a different phenomenon than the one described above, where the term referred to changes in the true seasonal component requiring an estimation procedure capable of detecting these changes. If the seasonal component is a function of the trend cycle component of the same series, then an estimation procedure that assumes the components are independent will yield biased estimates of the moving seasonal factors. The seasonal decline in unemployment, for example, is said to be milder when the level of unemployment is low than otherwise because firms are reluctant to temporarily discharge workers at a time when the labor force is fully employed. The appropriate seasonal factor will therefore vary between periods of high and low unemployment. Unlike the other reason for moving seasonals, this one does not involve a change in the relation among the components of the series (sometimes called the structure of the series) but simply a more complicated relation among them.

During the four decades preceding the Federal Reserve Act of 1913, a problem analogous to that alleged for unemployment prevailed on interest rates and the components of the money stock, although with consequences much more severe than the computation of biased estimates of seasonal factors. In his study written for the National Monetary Commission organized in response to the panic of 1907,[14] Kemmerer concluded that the greater incidence of banking panics in the fall than at other times of the year was due not to the normal seasonal tightness in the fall money market but to that tightness coming at the same time as a cyclical crisis. The seasonal movement, in effect, played the role of the proverbial straw.[15]

[13] Mendershausen, *op. cit.*, pp. 254–262.

[14] See also Milton Friedman and Anna Jacobson Schwartz, *A Monetary History of the United States, 1867–1960,* Princeton for NBER, 1963, pp. 171–172.

[15] The evidence on this point is mixed. Kemmerer found that "of the eight panics which have occurred since 1873 [as of 1910], four occurred in the fall or early winter (i.e., those of 1873, 1890, 1899, and 1907); three broke out in May (i.e., those of 1884, 1893, and 1901); and one (i.e., that of 1903) extended from March until well along in November." After discussing the "minor panics or 'panicky periods,' " he concludes that "The evidence accordingly points to a tendency for the panics to occur during the seasons normally characterized by a stringent money market." (*Op. cit.*, p. 232.)

Even if the seasonal component, expressed as a ratio to the moving average, were systematically related to the level of the moving average (or trend-cycle component) the estimated seasonal factors would not reveal this relation. Since the factors are computed from averages of the SI ratios across years, the variation of the SI ratios due to the cyclical variation is canceled out in the averaging process. In the case of an extreme cyclical movement, a related seasonal movement would likely result in an SI ratio that would be regarded as an extreme observation and be eliminated from the computation of the seasonal estimates. However, any relation that exists between the seasonal and cyclical components would present itself in a time series of the SI ratios. Chapter 3 considers this point.

Even in the absence of a true relation between the seasonal and cyclical components the inappropriate use of either an additive or multiplicative adjustment, that is, the use of one when the other is required, will result in an apparent relation between the seasonal and cyclical components.

When the level of rates is low the basis point equivalent of a multiplicative adjustment factor is smaller than when the level of rates is high. If the true seasonality were additive, and a multiplicative adjustment method were used, there would result an inverse relation between the SI ratios and the level of rates. Assume, for example, the true seasonal difference for a particular month to be 50 basis points. If in estimating the seasonal variation a multiplicative method were used, the SI ratio computed for this month would be high when the level of rates were, say, 100 basis points (i.e., 150/100) and low when the level were, say, 400 basis points (i.e., 450/400). Application of this test to the computed SI ratios for the Treasury bill rates does not reveal a systematic inverse relation between these ratios and the level of rates. However, the opposite procedure designed to test the efficacy of a multiplicative adjustment, assuming the true seasonal were multiplicative and the estimates additive, fails to confirm the appropriateness of a multiplicative adjustment. The question is therefore open and invites deference to convention—which is to use a multiplicative adjustment unless an additive one is clearly indicated.[16]

There is a method that combines elements of both the additive

[16] See Julius Shiskin and Harry Eisenpress, *Seasonal Adjustment by Electronic Computer Methods,* New York, NBER Technical Paper No. 12, 1958, p. 434.

and multiplicative adjustment. Seasonal irregular ratios are computed for each month and the set for each month regressed on the trend cycle component for that month; twelve regressions in all. The constant term of each regression is an estimate of the additive component of that month's seasonal factor and the regression co-efficient of the multiplicative component. This method, however, assumes stable seasonality in the sense used earlier in this report.[17]

SEASONAL ADJUSTMENT ON COMPUTERS

The X-11 program, used in this study, embodies a series of refinements in the original ratio-to-moving average technique that Macaulay developed in the 1930's. By reducing the cost and virtually eliminating the tedium of the vast number of elementary calculations this method of adjustment requires, the program makes feasible the use of complex weighting schemes in computing moving averages that are both elastic (i.e., remain faithful to the original series) and smooth (i.e., avoid the irregular wiggles). It allows, moreover, the extensive use of iteration to mitigate the obscuring influence of the irregular component on the separation of the seasonal from the trend-cycle components. Its most important advantage is the reduction in the time cost and skills required in manual adjustments.

The program's advantages are particularly obvious through the stage in which the modified seasonal irregular ratios or differences are computed as, of course, are their mean values, or the stable seasonal factors, when relevant. An experienced draftsman, however, can graphically fit moving seasonals to the SI ratios as well as the program does, and probably better than the program does when the

[17] There is clearly room here for variations on a theme. One can adapt the regression method to allow for a moving seasonal by applying the regression method as stated and applying the X-11 method to the residuals of the regressions. In that case one could obtain: an additive component, a component related to the trend cycle, and a moving seasonal component. Since this study uncovered no evidence of a relation between the seasonal and trend-cycle components of the interest rate series there was no reason to experiment with this method. In his exhaustive article Mendershausen (op. cit.) describes many exotic techniques for circumventing this or that problem of conventional methods; virtually all of them are in desuetude either because they introduced other problems or they were too unwieldy.

series has a prominent irregular component. Moreover, judgment is often required in determining whether an adjustment for any subperiod should be undertaken at all. Since the analysis of variance is a test of the means of the SI ratios for the whole sample period, there is some danger that the presence of a relatively strong seasonal component in one subperiod will affect the means for the whole period sufficiently to lend an apparent significance to the computed differences among them. (This effect would have to be large enough to overcome the increased within-group variance as a result of the greater heterogeneity of the SI ratios of a given month that a moving seasonal implies.) The program adjusts the whole series regardless of the results of the analysis of variance. The user cannot rely on the F-test alone to decide whether to accept the adjustment in its entirety.

The absence of objective criteria for selecting the period of adjustment, the extent of the adjustment, or the quality of the results [18] precludes an elaborate tabulation of this study's findings replete with standard errors. Nevertheless, from the descriptive statistics, the diagrams, and the verbal entourage, patterns emerge that are worth noting. Chapter 3 presents this material for seventeen interest rate series.

[18] "A statistician who has struggled with seasonal adjustments of numerous time series is not likely to underestimate the part played by 'hunch' and 'judgment' in his operations." Burns and Mitchell, *op. cit.*, p. 44.

CHAPTER 3

———— ◆▶ ————

The Evidence of Seasonality in Interest Rates

INTRODUCTION

THIS CHAPTER EVALUATES the evidence of seasonality in postwar interest rates and suggests suitable adjustments where appropriate. The evaluation consists of graphically identifying biases in the SI ratios over or under the 100.0 level. While the one-way analysis of variance test for seasonality is a useful method for identifying systematic deviations of the SI ratios from 100.0, its reference to the entire period makes it ineffective as a means of distinguishing the subperiods with evidence of seasonality from those without it.[1] The consistent deviation of a given month's SI ratio in the same direction from the 100.0 line is strong evidence of seasonality regardless of the variation in the magnitude of these deviations, that is, in the seasonal amplitude. The evidence of seasonality is weak when there are constant reversals of direction or when the relationship among the patterns of SI ratios is generally unstable from year to year. The summary statistics that most computer programs for seasonal adjust-

[1] One can apply the analysis of variance to separate subperiods, but the problem of choosing the limits of the subperiods remains.

ment supply (such as the average month-to-month change in the seasonal component by itself or relative to that of the other components) do not help evaluate the evidence of seasonality since, aside from the analysis of variance test, they only summarize what the program has done. They do not provide independent measures of either the evidence of seasonality or the quality of the adjustment. Once the existence of a seasonal pattern is confirmed and the adjustment decided, then the summary statistics provide a useful summary of the results.

In seasonal analysis, as in regression analysis, one places greater confidence in tests for the existence of a relation than in its actual measurement. In addition to the problem of sampling error common to both analyses, the moving seasonal amplitude implies changing parameters and requires the adjustment method, in effect, to shoot at a moving target. Except for a few experiments this study does not originate any methods of adjustment, nor does it even compare the adjustments obtainable with existing methods.[2] Instead, charts of the seasonal factors obtained with the X-11 are superimposed on charts of the corresponding SI ratios to determine the method's success in capturing what appears to be the systematic movement of the SI ratios. There is no question but that one could fit by eye a curve that is more faithful than is the curve of factors to variation of the SI ratios; in the extreme, one could perfectly fit a curve to the SI ratios by simply connecting the points—that is, by simply treating them as the factors. The art of the adjustment is in identifying the *systematic* movement of the SI ratios. When the pattern of SI ratios is stable from year to year there is no problem; nor is there any when the seasonal amplitude changes gradually or the pattern evolves with an apparent method. But during transition periods, in which the series has strong irregular movements such as 1954 the SI ratios and estimated factors appear to be virtually unrelated. This study recommends ignoring the adjustment when the gap between the two is pervasive.

[2] The potential gain from these experiments is not, in this study's view, commensurate with the effort required.

SHORT-TERM SECURITIES

SUMMARY STATISTICS

Table 1 lists some of the summary statistics that are useful in describing the extent and significance of seasonal influence.[3] Columns 1–3 divide the total variance of the series into the parts due to each of the three components: the trend-cycle, seasonal, and irregular. These figures are analogous to readings from the spectral density function, which decomposes the variance of a time series according to the frequency of the recurring variation.[4] Column 4 lists the average month-to-month percentage changes (without regard to sign) of the seasonal component, and column 5 the ratio of column 4 to the corresponding statistics of the cyclical component. These figures, columns 1 through 5, strike averages for the whole study period, averages not of the true seasonal but of the estimated one, including a spill-over into periods without significant seasonality. Columns 7–10 give the dates and amplitudes of the highest and lowest seasonal factors observed during the study period.

But these figures may be only statistical artifacts; hence the need exists to ascertain their statistical significance. To partially satisfy this need, column 6 records the F-statistics.

The F-statistic may be low for any of several reasons, the enumeration of which will help in evaluating the charts that follow. The most important reason, of course, is the absence of any bias in the monthly SI ratios away from the mean value of 100.0; in other words, no

---

[3] The statistics are copied directly from the X-11 printout and are described more fully in the X-11 Manual, *op. cit.*

[4] Some recent studies have applied spectral analysis to the problem of identifying seasonal variation. While the principle is the same as that in the moving average method—to simultaneously or sequentially filter, or separate, different frequencies of variation—spectral analysis is a more sophisticated and more rigorous method of doing so. Some of the mathematical advantage is lost, however, in its application to a limited number of observations. This method, moreover, provides no direct adjustment for the seasonal and resembles, in this respect, analysis of variance instead of regression analysis. In his forthcoming study for the National Bureau, Tom Sargent applied spectral analysis to interest rates, among other financial variables, and reached conclusions virtually identical to those in the present study with respect to the extent and evolution of the seasonal in interest rates.

TABLE 1

Measures of the Relative Importance of the Seasonal Components of the Four Series of Short-Term Securities, 1948–65

Series	Percentage of Total Variance of Series Due to Each Component			Average Month-to-Month Percentage Changes Without Regard to Sign of Seasonal Component $\bar{S}$	Ratio of Column 4 to Corresponding Figures for the Cyclical Component $\bar{S}/\bar{C}$	F-Test for Stable Seasonality[b]	Date and Factor of Seasonal High and Low for Whole Period[c]			
							High		Low	
	I	C	S				Date	Factor (percentage)	Date	Factor (percentage)
	(1)	(2)	(3)	(4)	(5)	(6)	(7)	(8)	(9)	(10)
Yields on:										
91 day bills	37.72	42.52	19.76	2.54	0.68	9.662	Dec. 1957	113.9	July 1957	87.4
9–12 month securities	35.91	49.77	14.32	1.85	0.54	4.557	Dec. 1956	109.0	June 1957	90.7
Commercial paper[a]	35.38	42.98	21.64	1.81	.71	4.034	Dec. 1958	107.5	May 1959	92.8
Bankers' acceptances	24.57	49.39	26.04	2.07	.72	11.293	Dec. 1957	111.4	July 1956	89.3

[a] The sample period for commercial paper rates ends in June 1965.

[b] All ratios are statistically significant at the 5 per cent level.

[c] A moving seasonal component was estimated for both series. Columns 7 and 9 list the dates when the amplitudes of the seasonal variations were greatest and columns 8 and 10 the values of the estimated seasonal factors for these dates.

seasonality. But a low F-statistic does not imply the absence of seasonality over the whole sample period. The smaller the subperiod of true seasonality the greater the burden on this period's SI ratios to influence the means for the whole sample period and thereby enlarge the between means variance, the numerator of the F-ratio. The burden is aggravated by the fact that a moving seasonal component combines with the irregular component to enlarge the within-group variance, the denominator of the F-ratio. When, for example, the F-statistic is computed for long-term Treasury securities over the entire period, its value (1.787) signifies the absence of seasonality; whereas, when computed over the period 1955 through 1962 the result (4.726) confirms the presence of seasonality. Similarly, the F-statistic in Table 1 for nine- to twelve-month Treasury securities is low because the seasonal pattern before 1955 was at best highly irregular. When the seasonal pattern changes over the sample period, even when in each subperiod the pattern is unambiguous, the F-statistic suffers as the differences among the mean monthly SI ratios are reduced. Combine this problem with the fact that seasonal patterns do not change instantaneously but rather evolve through periods of transition during which a coherent pattern is virtually nonexistent. In the eighteen-year sample period the seasonal pattern of commercial paper rates underwent several changes, and the low F-statistic shown in Table 1 in part reflects this fact.[5] Finally, the F-statistic may be low not because there is no seasonality but because of a strong irregular component; the means of the SI ratios are different from 100.0, but the standard errors of the means are high. This condition applies to all the interest rate series and in particular to commercial paper rates and yields on municipal bonds. Here again the diagrams are essential for determining whether the seasonal pattern has sufficient stability to warrant adjustment.

At its highest the seasonal component pushes the Treasury bill rate 14 per cent (rounded to nearest integer) above its trend-cycle value; at its lowest, 13 per cent below. For a bill rate in the neighborhood of 4 per cent (i.e., 400 basis points) these seasonal factors correspond to about 50 basis points.[6] At 11 per cent on

[5] These changes are described later in the section.
[6] These figures are actually underestimates since they embody the dampening effects of the lower peak levels of adjacent years. Later in this chapter an experiment is described that exemplifies this point.

either side of the trend-cycle values, the peak seasonal amplitude for yields on bankers' acceptances is somewhat less. Relative to the total variation of the series, however, the seasonal component of the yields on bankers' acceptances is the most important of the four series, and its F-statistic is highest. The diagrams, to be discussed presently, support the conclusion that this series evinces the strongest seasonal component. The series for which the summary statistics are least reliable is the series on commercial paper rates, for which, in addition, the F-statistic is lowest. The diagrams will justify this conclusion as well.

TREASURY BILL RATES

Chart 7 plots the seasonal factors for Treasury bill rates super-imposed on the corresponding SI ratios. From a relative high in January the Treasury bill rate seasonal pattern typically declines past seasonally neutral February, downward through the spring months to its trough in June or July and then turns sharply upward through seasonally neutral August to September, from which it rises gradually to its peak in December.[7] Surprisingly, this pattern is quite apparent, although the amplitude is small, in 1948, when the Federal Reserve pegged the prices of Treasury bills within narrow limits. This curve is shown in the first panel of Chart 7 together with the unmodified SI ratios. In subsequent panels of Chart 7 the pattern is shown to dissolve until about 1953 and then gradually to emerge again, but with greater amplitude, in the middle fifties, keeping this shape into the sixties as its amplitude virtually disappeared. By 1965 there was little left but a 2 per cent trough in June–July and a 2 per cent peak in December–January.

The factor curves, the broken lines of Chart 7, are for the most part dampened versions of the corresponding SI ratios, although at times the factor curve for one year betrays the influence of its predecessor more than that of its contemporary SI ratios. In this regard the factor curves ignore certain abrupt movements of the SI ratios, as in April 1955, the program being designed to sidestep points it regards as extreme.[8]

---

[7] Before 1957 the movement between September and December was not monotonic.

[8] Briefly, an extreme point is one that falls outside the range of 1.5 standard deviations, the latter computed for the entire set of data several times to

CHART 7

SI Ratios and Seasonal Factors for Treasury Bill Rates, 1948–65

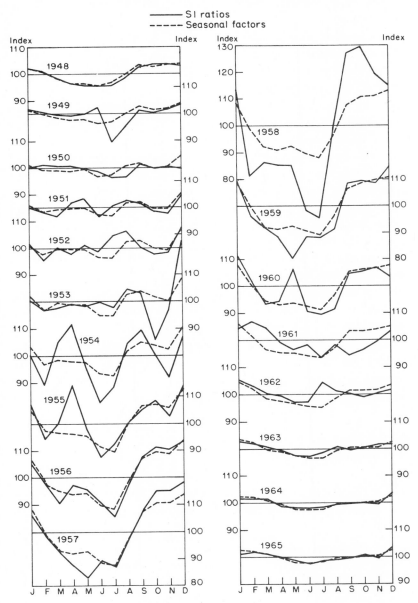

The relative stability of the seasonal pattern is in part a measure of the adjustment's effectiveness since the program does not attempt to directly fit the solid lines in Chart 7. Instead it smooths the SI ratios month by month as shown in Chart 8. As a given month's factors evolve through the years, any persistent change in their relation to another month's factors, that is, any change in the ordering of the twelve factors, will change the seasonal patterns given in Chart 7. Barring the extremes, the factor curves in Chart 8 fit the SI ratios quite closely although severely dampening their movement. One may wish to quarrel with the fit at a few places, but it will soon be shown that any reasonable alterations would have little quantitative importance. The two or three years preceding 1954 and following 1960 appear overly dependent on the years in between; and correspondingly, the peak period is excessively dampened. Aside from the transitional months, February and August, the monthly factor curves trace out the bell-shaped curves noted earlier, inverted in the low months, of course, and most of them remain above 100 or below 100 throughout the period. While most of the curves as of 1965 roughly coincide with the 100.0 line, the curves for July and December are still about 2 per cent under and over the line, denoting the persistence of a small seasonal variation in Treasury bill rates. However, the pattern for the last four years differs somewhat from that in earlier years: the trough appears in June instead of July; the January factors become at least as prominent as the ones for December; and, in the last two years, the November factors dip below the 100.0 line. Similar changes will be shown to have occurred in yields on bankers' acceptances as well.[9]

OTHER SHORT-TERM RATES

The seasonal patterns of the other short-term rates considered, except for commercial paper rates prior to 1956, are very similar to the one for Treasury bill rates. The similarity is greatest in the peak

eliminate the effect on it of the extreme points. The extremes are weighted linearly from 1 to 0 as they fall between 1.5 and 2.5 standard deviations. An extreme SI ratio different from 100 by two standard deviations is weighted 0.5. See X-11 Manual, *op. cit.*, pp. 4–5.

[9] The appendix to this chapter uses alternate adjustment procedures to evaluate the X-11 adjustment of Treasury bill rates.

CHART 8

Variation of Monthly Factor Curves and SI Ratios of Treasury Bill
Rates Through Years, 1948–65

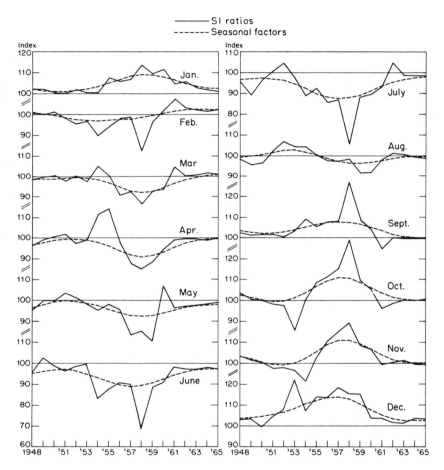

period, when the patterns for all the series have their greatest stability.
Table 2 lists the simple correlation coefficients between the twelve seasonal factors for Treasury bill rates and those for the other series over
selected years. In 1957 the correlations were all in excess of .95,
indicating virtual identity among the four patterns; by 1965, however,
the correlations were much less, and could be in part the spurious
aftermath of the earlier similarity.

TABLE 2

Sample Correlation Coefficients Between the Seasonal Factors
for Treasury Bill Rates and Those for Other Short-Term
Rates for Selected Years

	1953 (1)	1957 (2)	1963 (3)	1965 (4)
Bankers' acceptances	.6430	.9742	.7926	.5283
Commercial paper	.1380	.9724	.8917	n.a.
9−12 month Treasury securities	.8447	.9510	.7700	.6492

NOTE: The numbers are all simple correlation coefficients between
the seasonal factors of Treasury bill rates and the factors in the corresponding years for the other three series.
n.a. = not available.

Closest in pattern and evolution to that of Treasury bill rates is
the seasonal movement of yields on bankers' acceptances. As in the
case of bills, the seasonal pattern for yields on bankers' acceptances
is fairly stable from 1948 through 1950, but, again like bills, the fit
is less adequate from 1951 through 1954. In Chart 9 the estimated
factors are shown to grossly exaggerate the trough in July. Seasonality
exists in the period (July, for example, is always below the 100.0
line and December above), but its pattern is less stable than and
differs from the patterns of other years. During the peak period its
pattern is the familiar high in January, declining past neutral February
through the spring lows to a trough in July, then climbing steeply upward to September and, more gradually, to a December peak. Although its peak amplitude, at 12 per cent on either side of the corresponding trend-cycle values, is somewhat less than the peak in the
bill rate seasonal pattern, the seasonal amplitude on yields on bankers' acceptances is more prominent in the total variation of the series
(columns 3 and 5 of Table 1), and the estimated factors are more
faithful to the SI ratios (Chart 9). Beginning in 1959 the pattern
begins to change somewhat, the trough shifts from July to June and
the peak from December to January. These changes, as well as the dip
in November, are virtually identical to those that occurred somewhat
later in Treasury bill rates. Chart 9 reveals the low and declining

CHART 9

SI Ratios and Seasonal Factors for Bankers' Acceptance Rates, 1948–65

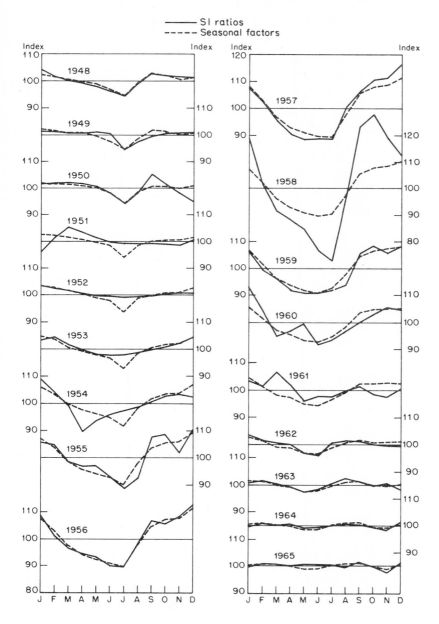

seasonal amplitude in yields on bankers' acceptances in the sixties. Although the last year of the adjustment period is always tricky, the factors for 1965 appear to signal the end of the seasonal component.

Because its pattern is less stable than the patterns of the two short-term series described above, the seasonal variation of commercial paper rates is more difficult to isolate. Chart 10 plots the SI ratios and corresponding factors for commercial paper rates. From 1948 through 1950 the seasonal pattern, except for a high in October, is virtually the mirror image of the pattern in the late fifties—the first half year in the earlier period being above the 100.0 line, the second half below. The pattern evolves through a transition period in 1951 to a pattern that extends through 1955, and is quite similar to the one for long-term rates. Beginning with a low in January the factors drop to a trough in March, turn up through May or June to a peak in October and then sharply down. The pattern in 1955 already blends into the new pattern that is characteristic of the other short-term series: From a high in January the factors turn down through neutral February and the springtime lows to a trough in July then go up through neutral August to a peak in December. This pattern persists throughout the period of peak seasonality in the late fifties, during which, however, the seasonal amplitude never exceeds 8 per cent of the corresponding average values of the series. Beginning in 1962 the pattern appears to drift back towards the earlier one that resembled the pattern of long-term series. Nevertheless, the seasonal amplitude persists through the end of the period.

As in the case of the other short-term series, there is a repetitive ripple in the yields on nine- to twelve-month Treasury securities from 1948 through 1950, but, as Chart 11 shows, the factors do not fit the SI ratios as well as in the case of the other short-term series. Several years of erratic movement follow before the final pattern emerges in 1955. Choppy at first, it evolves rapidly into full shape in 1957 and slowly down again but persisting through the end of the period. Indeed, in 1965 the amplitude is greater and the pattern more discernible than in the case of bill rates.

The pattern during the late fifties is very similar to that of the other short-term series except that the trough comes a month earlier (in June) and a fall plateau replaces the December peak. This change in pattern is in the direction of the long-term series.

CHART 10

SI Ratios and Seasonal Factors for Commercial Paper Rates, 1948–65

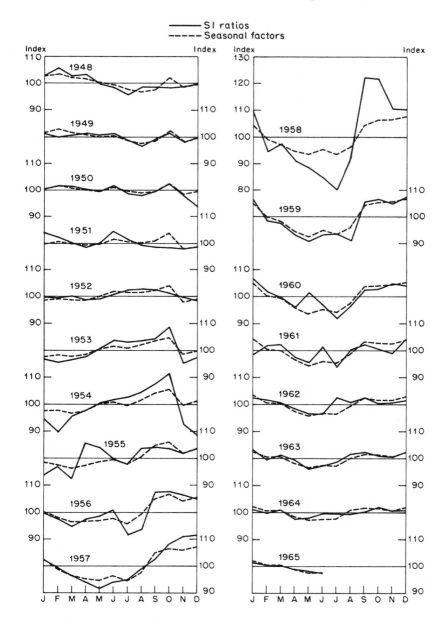

CHART 11

SI Ratios and Seasonal Factors for Yields on Nine- to Twelve-Month
U.S. Government Securities, 1948–65

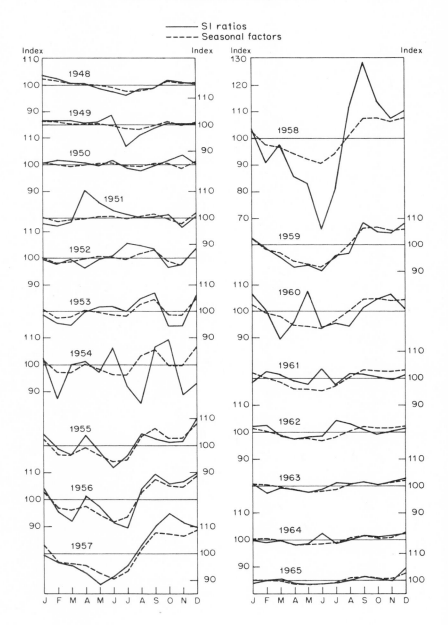

SUMMARY OF SHORT-TERM SERIES

While the seasonal patterns of short-term rates are not entirely uniform throughout the postwar period, for the most part they have in common springtime lows and a midyear trough, as well as fall highs and a December peak continuing with some diminution through January. This pattern describes all four series in the period of greatest seasonality, 1956 through 1960. Treasury bill rates and yields on bankers' acceptances sustain this pattern throughout the 1948–65 period although not with as much stability and amplitude as during the 1956–60 period. The patterns for commercial paper rates prior to 1956 are quite different from those of the other short-term rates and, in fact, resemble those of the long-term rates that are described below. There are actually two distinct patterns for commercial paper rates during 1948–55, a fact making the adjustment for this period of questionable value. While the pattern for nine- to twelve-month Treasury securities prior to 1955 is quite similar to the one for Treasury bills (column 1 of Table 2), the factors are not sufficiently faithful to the SI ratios, in this study's view, to warrant an adjustment. In the later period, however, the seasonal influence is unambiguous. Chart 12 plots the time series of seasonal factors of the four short-term series considered in this study.

After 1960 the seasonal amplitudes of all the short-term series rapidly decline. While some seasonality persists after 1963, an adjustment will unavoidably introduce some additional error into the series. Whether the elimination of the true seasonal is worth the increased danger of introducing error as a result of adjusting for a spurious seasonal factor is an issue the user must decide. Table 3 lists the periods during which, in this study's view, the seasonal is worth adjusting for.

LONG-TERM SECURITIES

SUMMARY STATISTICS

The seasonal amplitudes of yields on long-term bonds are not high. In only two of the thirteen cases listed in Table 4 does the highest estimated factor for a given bond exceed 4 per cent and in only four

CHART 12

Seasonal Factors for Short-Term Interest Series, 1948-65

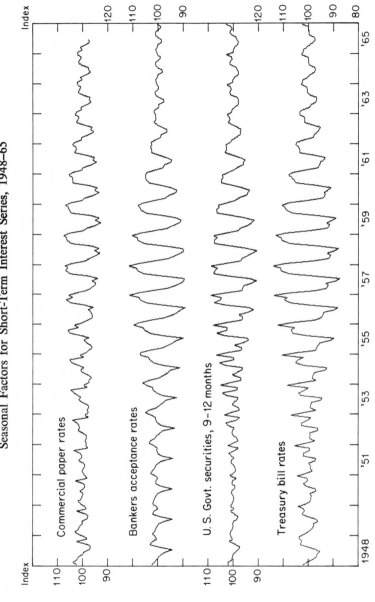

TABLE 3

Suggested Periods for Adjusting Short-Term Series

Security	Adjustment Period
Treasury bill rates	1948−65
Bankers' acceptance rates	1948−63
Commercial paper rates	1956−65
9−12 month Treasury security rates	1955−65

cases 3 per cent (column 8). Notwithstanding the low amplitudes, the computed F-statistics signify stable seasonality in all but two cases and in most cases by a wide margin (column 6). Finally, again notwithstanding the low peak amplitudes, as well as the seasonal components' relatively low average month-to-month percentage changes without regard to sign (column 4), the estimated percentages of total variation of the series due to the seasonal components (column 3) are roughly comparable and a little higher than the corresponding figure for Treasury bill rates.

These summary statistics are likely to be more reliable than the corresponding statistics for short-term securities because in the long-term bond rates, exclusive of the two Treasury series, the seasonality persisted throughout most of the study period, although with some changes in both pattern and amplitude. The summary statistics for three- to five-year and long-term Treasury securities, however, largely reflect the seasonal flourish in the late fifties. Both its small amplitude and its shifting pattern likely contribute to the persistence of seasonality in long-term bonds (as of 1965 the seasonal influence in most of the series was minute but discernible) since these characteristics in effect obscure the seasonal variation and thereby lessen the likelihood of investors trading them away.[10]

[10] A small amplitude does not by itself impugn the significance of the seasonal component. The seasonal amplitude for the series on the stock of money, for example, is never more than 3 per cent; although the value of the F-statistic in the postwar period is a robust 281. A comparison between column 5 in Tables 1 and 4 shows that relative to the variation of the cyclical component the seasonal amplitude of long-term bond rates is typically greater than that of short-term rates.

TABLE 4

Measures of the Relative Importance of the Seasonal Components in the Variation of Yields on Long-Term Bonds, 1948–65

Series	Percentage of Total Variation of Series Due to Each Component			Average Month-to-Month Percentage Changes Without Regard to Sign of Seasonal Component S	Ratio of Column 4 to Corresponding Figures for the Cyclical Component S/C	F-Test for Stable Seasonality	Date and Factor of Seasonal High and Low for Whole Period[a]			
							High		Low	
	I	C	S				Date	Factor (percentage)	Date	Factor (percentage)
	(1)	(2)	(3)	(4)	(5)	(6)	(7)	(8)	(9)	(10)
Municipals[b]										
highest rating	44.23	34.78	21.00	1.18	0.78	2.855[c]	Sept. 1958	104.7	Feb. 1958	96.6
lowest rating	45.97	36.30	17.72	0.86	0.70	1.515	Sept. 1958	102.3	Apr. 1960	97.7
high grade (Standard & Poor)	55.38	26.74	17.88	1.05	0.82	2.390[c]	Sept. 1958	103.5	Feb. 1955	07.1
Railroads										
highest rating	34.65	45.46	19.89	0.44	0.66	7.230[c]	Sept. 1957	101.8	Mar. 1957	98.3
lowest rating	36.92	38.36	24.71	0.59	0.81	7.111[c]	Dec. 1956	101.6	Mar. 1954	97.9

Series	Percentage of Total Variation of Series Due to Each Component			Average Month-to-Month Percentage Change Without Regard to Sign of Seasonal Component $\bar{S}$	Ratio of Column4 to Corresponding Figures for the Cyclical Component $\bar{S}/\bar{C}$	F-Test for Stable Seasonality	Date and Factor of Seasonal High and Low for Whole Period[a]			
							High		Low	
	I	C	S				Date	Factor (percentage)	Date	Factor (percentage)
	(1)	(2)	(3)	(4)	(5)	(6)	(7)	(8)	(9)	(10)
Corporates										
highest rating	37.74	38.63	23.62	.54	.78	5.806[c]	Sept. 1957	102.2	Mar. 1957	97.5
lowest rating	31.34	45.72	22.94	.43	.72	7.851[c]	Oct. 1957	101.7	Mar. 1955	98.5
Public Utilities										
highest rating	34.60	38.92	26.48	0.61	0.82	7.290[c]	Oct. 1958	103.2	Mar. 1958	97.2
lowest rating	38.26	41.22	20.52	0.44	0.70	7.078[c]	Oct. 1957	101.7	Mar. 1955	98.5
Industrials										
highest rating	46.42	29.75	23.83	0.66	0.89	4.130[c]	Sept. 1957	102.3	Mar. 1958	97.6
lowest rating	29.12	53.34	17.54	0.36	0.57	6.974[c]	Oct. 1957	101.4	Mar. 1958	98.6
U.S. Treasury										
long-term	7.51	40.42	2.08	0.50	0.55	1.787	Sept. 1957[b]	102.8	Apr. 1957	98.0
3–5 years	3.73	37.76	8.51	1.45	0.71	3.642[c]	Sept. 1957	105.8	Apr. 1959	95.2

Although there is a general bell-shaped pattern to the seasonal amplitudes of the long-term securities during the postwar period, the relative rise in the late fifties is not as pronounced as in the case of the short-term securities nor is it as pronounced in the private long-term rates as in the Treasury rates. Table 5 lists the variances of the seasonal factors of a given year for selected years for all the securities considered in this study. The variance of the twelve monthly factors is a convenient measure of the over-all seasonal amplitude for a given year. The bell-shaped pattern refers to the increase in the securities from 1953 to 1957 and their decrease to 1963. (The bell is actually quite symmetrical, a fact that is hidden by the different spans of the two periods.) Except for the railroad (lowest quality) securities, the table supports the generalization stated above.

There is a curious consistency in the relations among the seasonal factors of the several long-term series, a consistency for which there is no mechanical explanation. In Table 5, for example, the seasonal amplitude in 1954 for yields on lowest rated security groups is in every case less than the amplitude for the corresponding highest rated group; except for railroad bonds, this relationship holds in 1963 and 1965 as well.[11] Table 6 lists the correlation coefficients for the twelve monthly factors in 1957 of each of the long-term groups of securities with those of each of the other groups. In almost all cases the coefficients exceed .7; in most they exceed .8; and in many they exceed .9. The high correlations denote the substantial uniformity in the seasonal patterns of the long-term yields during the period of peak seasonality. Moreover, in virtually every case the correlation between

[11] Column 3 of Table 4 shows that the seasonal accounts for a smaller part of the total variation of low quality than of high quality bonds and the cyclical component accounts for a higher proportion (except for rails). This study is unable to explain the phenomenon.

NOTES TO TABLE 4

[a] A moving seasonal component was estimated for the four series. Columns 7 and 9 list the dates when the amplitudes of the seasonal component was greatest and columns 8 and 10 the values of the estimated seasonal factors for these dates.

[b] The estimated seasonal factor for September 1958 was also 102.8.

[c] Significant at 1 per cent level.

TABLE 5

*Variance of Seasonal Factors of a Given Year for Selected Years
for All Securities Considered in this Study*

Security	1953	1957	1963	1965
Long-Term bonds				
Municipals				
highest rating	2.789	6.386	1.395	1.279
lowest rating	1.182	2.085	0.734	0.605
high-grade (Standard & Poor)	2.914	3.614	1.624	1.445
Corporates				
highest rating	0.516	2.208	0.224	0.145
lowest rating	0.664	1.132	0.071	0.053
Industrials				
highest rating	0.557	2.286	0.398	0.302
lowest rating	0.588	1.014	0.112	0.075
Railroads				
highest rating	0.386	1.350	0.115	0.062
lowest rating	1.300	0.846	0.211	0.223
Public Utilities				
highest rating	0.762	3.580	0.260	0.144
lowest rating	0.381	2.490	0.094	0.075
U.S. Treasury				
long-term	0.231	2.161	0.253	0.096
3–5 years	2.756	14.455	0.992	0.308
Short-Term securities				
U.S. Treasury bills	15.453	92.910	5.080	2.996
Commercial paper	5.684	25.341	4.252	n.a.
Bankers' acceptances	12.816	67.158	1.603	0.734
U.S. Treasury 9–12 months	6.843	42.367	2.425	1.977

NOTE: Each number signifies the variance of the twelve seasonal factors computed separately for each of the years and securities shown.
n.a. = not available.

any group of securities, say corporates and industrials, is greater for comparisons among security groups of the same quality rating. Along the last row, for example, the correlation between the factors for the

TABLE 6

Coefficients of Correlation Among the Seasonal Factors in 1957 for All the Long-Term Securities Considered

Series	Municipals			Corporates		Industrials		U.S. Treasury		Railroads		Public Utilities	
	high-grade (Standard & Poor)	highest rating	lowest rating	highest rating	lowest rating	highest rating	lowest rating	long-term	3–5 years	highest rating	lowest rating	highest rating	lowest rating
Municipals													
highest rating	.9627												
lowest rating	.9385	.9596											
Corporates													
highest rating	.9644	.9349	.9134										
lowest rating	.7226	.7040	.7568	.8263									
Industrials													
highest rating	.9749	.9307	.9067	.9660	.7223								
lowest rating	.7320	.7178	.7529	.8196	.9765	.7237							
U.S. Treasury													
long-term	.9222	.9153	.8942	.8793	.7708	.8438	.8062						
3–5 years	.6553	.8514	.8163	.9036	.7914	.8440	.8251	.9400					
Railroads													
highest rating	.9370	.8943	.9036	.9568	.8654	.8923	.8559	.9163	.9346				
lowest rating	.7920	.6986	.7568	.8752	.9126	.8084	.9168	.7567	.8334	.8993			
Public Utilities													
highest rating	.9156	.9194	.8980	.9741	.8905	.9057	.8749	.8860	.9015	.9469	.8597		
lowest rating	.6860	.7252	.7452	.7967	.9650	.6962	.9512	.7435	.7369	.8015	.8152	.8774	

NOTE: Each coefficient, based on twelve observations, is computed by cross correlating the twelve factors of the vertical and horizontal series. Diagonal elements are omitted.

lowest rated version of the public utility group and those for, say, industrials-lowest rating, is greater than the correlation between the former and industrials-highest rating. In the row above, the correlations between the factors for the highest rated public utility group are greater in cases where the highest rated version of the paired group is considered in place of the lowest rated version of the same group. The correlations, of course, are not as high in years outside the period of peak seasonality; nor is the characteristic just described as conspicuous. These figures are shown in Tables 7 and 8.

By far the lowest correlations are with the long-term Treasury securities in 1965. These low coefficients help substantiate the conclusion that there is no seasonality in the series at the end of the study period. Evidence of uniformity is never more than suggestive. However, the more uniformity, the greater are the similarities among independently calculated results and the less likely are explanations of any given result that depend on alleged accidents or quirks in the computation. In this sense the similarity of the seasonal patterns and the curious relations among security groups of homogeneous rating constitute *prima facie* cases for the existence of a seasonal pattern, indictments, so to speak, on which it now behooves this study to obtain a conviction.

Before 1955 the typical seasonal pattern for yields on long-term securities describes low points in the first four months of the year and highs for the remainder, excepting a slight dip below 100.0 in November. The trough usually appeared in February or March, while the peak varied between July and December. The pattern changed in the 1954–56 period to one with a slight high in January, a rapid fall to a trough usually in March, continued lows through July, then a steep incline to a peak in September, and finally a gradual decline to December, still above the line. Table 9 lists the average seasonal factors for yields in long-term securities for selected years, computed by arithmetically averaging, the monthly factors for a given year, one at a time, of the thirteen long-term series. The recorded January factor, for example, is the average of all the January factors for the given year. In addition to the change in the seasonal pattern, the differences in the seasonal amplitude between the peak period in the late fifties and that before and after the period are revealed as well.

While Table 9 adequately describes the general seasonal pattern, its

TABLE 7

Coefficients of Correlation Among the Seasonal Factors in 1953 for All the Long-Term Securities Considered

Series	Municipals high-grade (Standard & Poor)	Municipals highest rating	Municipals lowest rating	Corporates highest rating	Corporates lowest rating	Industrials highest rating	Industrials lowest rating	U.S. Treasury long-term	U.S. Treasury 3–5 years	Railroads highest rating	Railroads lowest rating	Public Utilities highest rating
Municipals												
highest rating	.9609											
lowest rating	.7981	.8087										
Corporates												
highest rating	.8679	.7863	.7454									
lowest rating	.7224	.5943	.5041	.8114								
Industrials												
highest rating	.8880	.8268	.8020	.9185	.5921							
lowest rating	.6384	.5045	.4577	.7622	.9669	.5380						
U.S. Treasury												
long-term	.7881	.7092	.8303	.7772	.6281	.7944	.5338					
3–5 years	.3472	.1879	.3052	.6097	.5854	.4269	.5906	.5879				
Railroads												
highest rating	.7056	.5705	.4289	.8722	.9021	.7061	.8373	.5518	.5505			
lowest rating	.7316	.6001	.5127	.8660	.9774	.6681	.9407	.6040	.5792	.9619		
Public Utilities												
highest rating	.8468	.7739	.7470	.9737	.8165	.8522	.7907	.7718	.6739	.8037	.8382	
lowest rating	.5580	.4714	.4266	.6534	.9171	.3765	.9331	.4897	.6088	.7142	.8548	.7272

NOTE: Same as Table 6.

TABLE 8

Coefficients of Correlation Among the Seasonal Factors in 1965 for All the Long-Term Securities Considered

Series	Municipals			Corporates		Industrials		U.S. Treasury		Railroads		Public Utilities
	high-grade (Standard & Poor)	highest rating	lowest rating	highest rating	lowest rating	highest rating	lowest rating	long-term	3–5 years	highest rating	lowest rating	highest rating
Municipals												
highest rating	.8655											
lowest rating	.8308	.7063										
Corporates												
highest rating	.6837	.7054	.8218									
lowest rating	.7762	.7062	.8174	.9384								
Industrials												
highest rating	.5769	.5751	.6732	.9535	.8958							
lowest rating	.5012	.5032	.3760	.6152	.6248	.6149						
U.S. Treasury												
long-term	-.0939	-.3798	-.0377	-.1206	.0191	.0169	-.4666					
3–5 years	.2306	.0658	.5929	.5911	.5510	.6210	.1167	.5138				
Railroads												
highest rating	.3308	.1636	.6548	.6029	.5654	.5585	.1542	.2523	.8091			
lowest rating	.7303	.6211	.8418	.8538	.9189	.7912	.3435	.1191	.5646	.6900		
Public Utilities												
highest rating	.7939	.7504	.8317	.9216	.8983	.8833	.6508	-.1121	.4939	.3914	.7607	
lowest rating	.5433	.3077	.4219	.6064	.7205	.7434	.4972	.4636	.5530	.4100	.5857	.6382

NOTE: Same as Table 6.

TABLE 9

*Average Seasonal Factors for Yields on Long-Term
Securities for Selected Years*

	1953	1957	1963	1965
January	99.3	100.4	100.1	99.8
February	98.7	98.4	99.6	99.5
March	98.8	97.9	99.3	99.6
April	99.3	98.3	99.3	99.5
May	100.4	98.6	99.3	99.4
June	101.1	99.2	100.0	100.0
July	100.7	99.4	100.4	100.4
August	100.5	103.1	100.3	100.2
September	101.1	102.5	100.7	100.6
October	100.5	101.9	100.5	100.4
November	99.8	101.2	100.3	100.1
December	100.4	101.0	100.4	100.3

NOTE: The figures for each month are computed by arithmetically averaging the seasonal factors for that month of the thirteen long-term securities considered in this study.

evolution, and the order of magnitude involved, it necessarily obscures important differences in the several series. The high correlations in Table 6 reveal a similarity in the patterns of most series during the late fifties; although the considerable differences in amplitude revealed in Table 5 are not, of course, accounted for. The somewhat lower correlations in 1953 and the considerably lower ones in 1965 lessen the usefulness of the computed average pattern outside the 1955–60 period. In addition to the variety of patterns and amplitudes in the long-term series, there are also differences in the quality of the estimates of the seasonal factors. To decide on the extent of appropriate adjustment for each series it is therefore necessary to examine the familiar charts of factors and SI ratios, which we do now.

GRAPHIC ANALYSIS OF SEASONAL VARIATION

U.S. Treasury securities.   Chart 13 plots the seasonal factors and SI ratios for long-term U.S. Treasury securities (the scale is twice

53

CHART 13

SI Ratios and Seasonal Factors for Yields on Long-Term U.S. Bonds,
1948–65

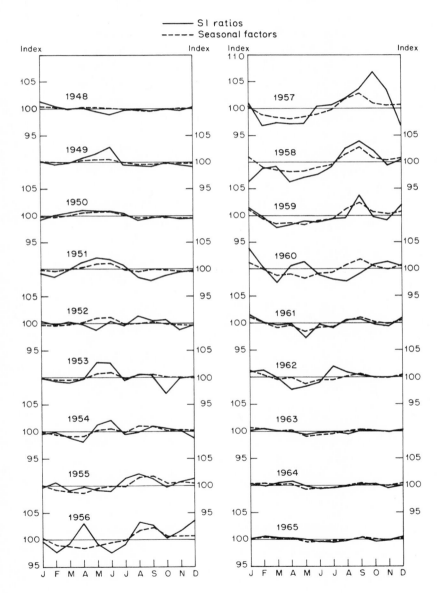

that used for short-term securities). The pattern prior to 1953 is very similar to the early pattern of commercial paper rates; the peak coming in midyear and the trough in the fall. Although the amplitude is small, the pattern is quite real. The reason for the asserted reality resides not only in the similarity between the curves connecting the SI ratios and the ones connecting the factors but also in the position of the factors, falling as they do between the SI ratios and the 100.0 level. The latter result is most conspicuous for 1951 and has the effect of both dampening the adjusted series and minimizing the possibility of the adjustment contributing to the random fluctuation of the series. As in the case of the Treasury bill rates during the late fifties, the assurance that all that is removed is seasonal comes at the expense of understating what seasonal influence there is. The data for 1952 provide a good example of the dilemma involved in adjusting a series with a rapidly shifting pattern: the two curves are virtually unrelated. Use of the estimated factors may then introduce random errors into the series. In 1953 the pattern assumes the shape of the average pattern of Table 9 and, hence, the high correlations in Table 7 between the long-term Treasuries and the other securities. In the following years the pattern rapidly bends into the one typical of all the rates in the late fifties. Even in this period the fit is not very good, although the pattern is clearly there; and the amplitude is among the highest of the long-term security groups. One notices, even in the late fifties, how the low part of the pattern is gradually extended through the summer, as with the short-term securities. By 1965 the pattern is very different from the average pattern and, in fact, inversely correlated with those of most of the long-term series (Table 8). It is clear, then, that the low F-statistic noted earlier for this series is due both to a constantly shifting pattern resulting in a mediocre fit and an unstable pattern even within the periods it describes. That a seasonal pattern existed in the late fifties and even that a systematic ripple persisted to the end of the study period is, in this study's view, established. Whether there is reasonable cause to adjust the series outside the 1955–59 period is somewhat dubious; and whether it would be meaningful to adjust a series for such a short period is equally dubious. This series is perhaps one that may profitably be left alone.

Chart 14 plots the seasonal factors and SI ratios for U.S. Treasury

CHART 14

SI Ratios and Seasonal Factors for Yields on U.S. Government
Three- to Five-Year Securities, 1948–65

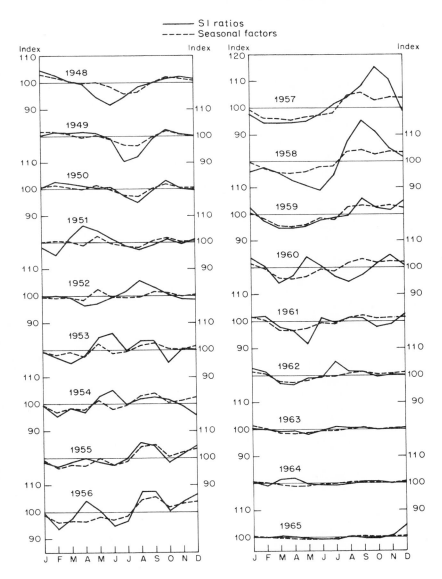

securities with three- to five-year maturities. There is a fairly clear pattern for the years 1948–60 followed by several years of erratic movement—the pattern for 1953 is typical. In 1955 the pattern assumes the shape it maintains for the remainder of the decade. In this period the seasonal amplitude of this series is somewhere between the typical amplitude of short- and long-term securities. From 1960 on, however, the seasonal pattern is too unstable to justify an adjustment.

Municipal securities.   Of all the long-term securities the F-statistics are among the lowest and the amplitudes among the highest for the yields on the three municipal bond series considered. The F-statistics, however, are not brought down, as in the case of long-term Treasuries, by constantly shifting patterns of small amplitude and erratic transition periods; nor is the F-statistic spuriously high as a result of the attenuation of the peak seasonal in the late fifties. Chart 15 plots the seasonal factors and SI ratios for yields on municipal bonds of highest rating. Excluding the first two years, the pattern in the early years is quite similar to the general pattern of this period described in Table 9: lows during the first four months, a June peak, but then, unlike the general pattern, a rapid decline to lows in the last two months. The large gaps between the curves, implied in the unusually large irregular component recorded in column 1 of Table 4, reflect changes in the seasonal amplitude of the series rather than an unstable pattern. Although the greater dispersion of a given month's SI ratios results in less reliable estimates of the seasonal factors, the diagrams reveal the SI ratios for given months to fluctuate about means that clearly remain above or remain below the 100.0 line. From 1949 through 1954, every June is a high, and every January and December are lows. In 1955 the new pattern emerges, again similar to the general pattern of the late fifties, with a trough in February or March and a peak in September. The pattern changes somewhat after 1959, but persists in similar form through the end of the study period.

In this case, therefore, and in the case of the other municipal groups not shown here, a basis for seasonal adjustment exists in spite of the feeble F-statistics. There is an important difference between the effects of random variations in seasonal amplitude and those in the seasonal pattern on identifying the presence of seasonality. In the

CHART 15

SI Ratios and Seasonal Factors for Yields on Municipal Bonds, Highest
Rating, 1948–65

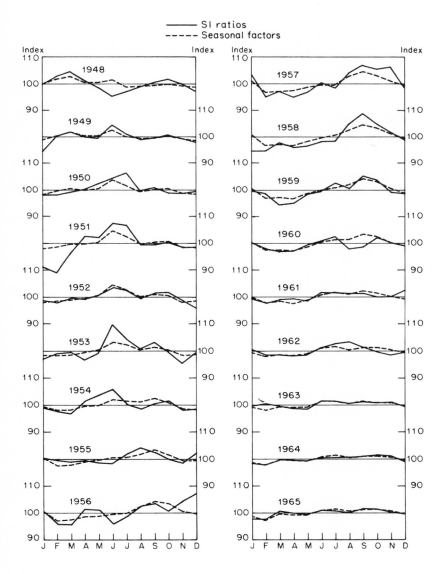

former case, by narrowly defining extreme points, the program can dampen the estimated seasonal amplitudes, imposing a downward bias on the estimated means, and thereby reducing the risk of wrongly affirming the presence of seasonality. In the latter case the danger is greater that the program will impose a seasonal pattern on the series.

Private long-term securities. Although there are differences in detail it is convenient to describe the seasonality of yields on private long-term securities for the group as a whole. This group's seasonal pattern differs from that of the municipals by its somewhat smaller amplitude and its greater stability. Table 4 records higher *F*-statistics, lower residual variation, and smaller peak amplitudes (columns 6, 1, 8, and 9 respectively), and Table 5 shows the seasonal amplitudes of the private groups to be less than those of the municipals with very few exceptions throughout the study period.[12] The curves connecting the SI ratios in Chart 16, drawn for yields on corporate securities of lowest rating, are clearly less choppy than the corresponding curves for municipal securities, and the amplitude of the corporates is smaller. The patterns are somewhat erratic through 1951, but thereafter they are quite similar to the first pattern listed in Table 9. In 1955 the January factor starts to rise and the low period extends into the summer, typical of the general pattern in this period. This pattern persists to the end of the study period although its amplitude at the end is barely perceptible.

The stability of the pattern and therefore the evidence of seasonality is further illustrated in Chart 17, where the SI ratios and the factors are plotted one month at a time across the years. There are five months for which the direction of seasonal change is consistent throughout the study period: March, April, September, October, and November. Beginning in 1950 the SI ratios for March are consistently below the 100.0 line; their amplitudes in the early fifties are as great as in the late fifties, tapering off in 1960 but persisting to the end of the study period. The factor curve is virtually identical with the curve connecting the SI ratios. Again for April, the SI ratios remain consistently below the 100.0 level, crossing it briefly in 1951 and

---

[12] It may be that an explanation of the difference in amplitude between the two groups of securities lies in the greater ease with which private corporations can time their borrowing to correspond with periods of seasonally low yields.

CHART 16

SI Ratios and Seasonal Factors for Yields on Corporate Bonds, Lowest
Rating, 1948–65

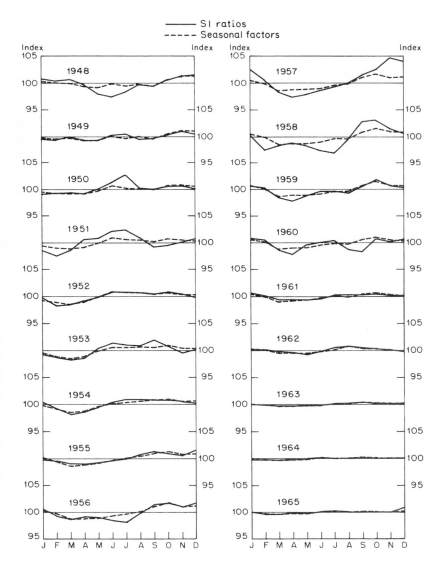

CHART 17

SI Ratios and Seasonal Factors for Yields on Corporate Bonds, Lowest
Rating, One Month at a Time, 1948–65

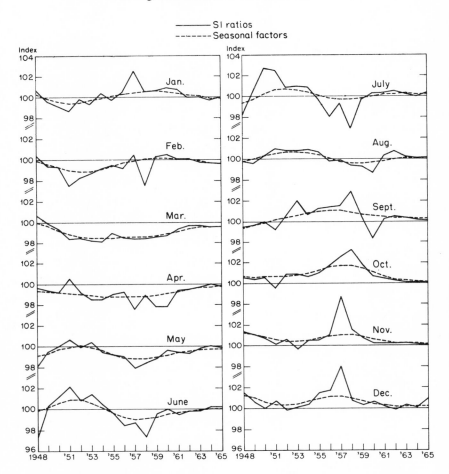

again in 1961. Except for these two years the factor curve either
coincides with the SI curve or rises above it, in any case it does not
exaggerate the seasonal variation. In September, barring 1951 and
1960, and again in October the SI ratios are consistently above 100.0.
Of the four months only October evinces a greater amplitude in the
late fifties; and the factor curve virtually nullifies the increase. The
curves for the middle months, May through August, and the one for

January all cross the 100.0 line at about 1954, signifying the changed pattern.

While there are differences in the patterns of the various groups of long-term securities a detailed account of each of the series would be almost as tedious to write as it would be to read. In lieu of that Chart 18 plots time series of the seasonal factors for all the long-term series considered in this study.

SUMMARY OF LONG-TERM BONDS

In spite of the low seasonal amplitudes in long-term bonds, both the summary statistics and the diagrams confirm the presence of seasonality in these series throughout most of the sample period. Starting about 1950, the seasonal factors are typically below the 100.0 line in the first four months of the year, the trough usually occurring in March, rise above the line in midyear and beyond it to a peak in September or October then fall back to the 100.0 line in November and December. Starting in 1955 the midyear months stay below the 100.0 line, and the months at either end rise a little. The key seasonal months—March, April, September, and October—are largely unaffected by this change. The prominent bell-shaped pattern in the seasonal factors described for the short-term rates is less prominent in the case of long-term bonds, although the seasonal factors for some of the series clearly evolve in this manner.

As in the other series considered in this study there are some years for which there appear to be no seasonal movement at all or for which, whether present or not, the seasonal is too small and uncertain to be measured. There is no accepted method for reliably choosing the years for which an adjustment is appropriate. Nor do the necessary conditions prevail for reliable inference from the summary statistics. Although there is a large subjective element involved in the method used in this study, the primary criterion has been the apparent stability in the seasonal patterns regardless of their amplitudes. But the judgment involved in this study is restricted to the choice of accepting the results of the X-11 program. Additional judgment is required to improve this adjustment. Table 10 presents the suggested dates for accepting the machine adjustment. For convenience the table includes the findings for all seventeen series considered in this study.

CHART 18

Seasonal Factors for Long-Term Interest Rates, 1948–65

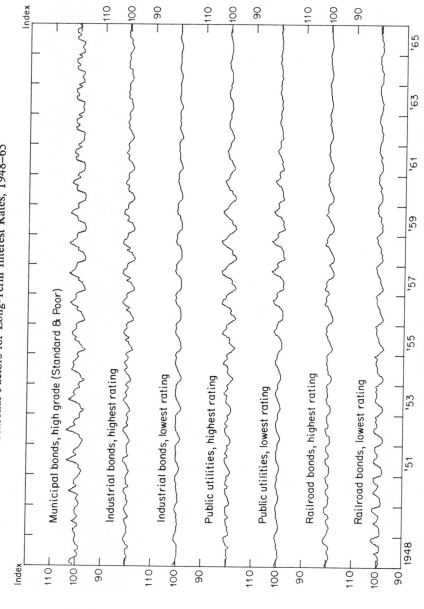

variation, the choice of the appropriate adjustment depends on which of the two concepts of a seasonal movement is intended.

To illustrate the practical significance of this issue the study experimented with alternate adjustments of Treasury bill rates. The Kuznets amplitude ratio method of adjustment is convenient for dealing with an abruptly changing seasonal amplitude provided the month-to-month pattern of factors is fixed, and only the amplitude changes from year to year. The factors are computed by regressing, one year at a time, the twelve modified SI ratios [14] on the set of constant factors obtained by averaging, one month at a time, the modified SI ratios over the whole period. The more similar the particular year's pattern is to the average pattern the higher will be the correlation coefficient; when it is equal to one the regression coefficient will exactly measure the proportionate difference in amplitude between them.[15] Table 11 lists the coefficients of correlation and regression, as well as the latter's t-value for the eighteen regressions from 1948 through 1965. All three statistics reveal the bell-shaped pattern in the seasonal amplitude that was noted earlier. Again, the seasonal in 1948 is unusually clear, its pattern being highly correlated with the average pattern. In the following two years the seasonal is still inexplicably strong, although less than in 1948, the pegged prices notwithstanding. After two dormant years in 1951 and 1952 the seasonal emerges again in 1953 and more strongly in 1954, although the erratic pattern noted earlier is reflected in a correlation coefficient that is lower than in the following years. The peak seasonal continues through 1960, after which it drops off sharply; and after 1961 the seasonal is very small.

The regression coefficients listed in Table 11 are convenient for evaluating the hypothesis that there is a relation between the sea-

[14] That is, modified to eliminate extreme values. It is clearly important to eliminate the effect of extreme values on a regression computed with twelve observations, although the X-11 modifications, used here, will in some cases dampen the very changes in amplitude the Kuznets method is designed to reveal.

[15] In commenting on this method Burns and Mitchell (*op. cit.*, pp. 48–49), recommend not accepting the estimate when the correlation coefficient falls below .7. It is clear that when the pattern changes, as in the case of commercial paper rates, the method has no value. The pattern for bill rates, however, is fairly stable; therefore, a low correlation coefficient signifies doubtful seasonality.

sonal and cyclical components. Chapter 2 noted that the X-11 method of smoothing the SI ratios over adjacent years to compute the factors necessarily obscures any relation that may exist between its seasonal and cyclical components. There is nothing, however, to prevent the Kuznets amplitude-ratios (the regression coefficients in Table 11) from varying with the cyclical component of the series. There is clearly nothing in columns 3 and 7 to reveal any relation between the prominence of the seasonal component and the level of the series as shown in Chart 19. The erratic movements in the SI ratios in 1954 and 1958 suggest that the irregular component may be more prominent during cyclical troughs, a proposition that may or may not reflect on the capacity of the Henderson curve to capture sharp turning points.

Columns 4 and 8 of Table 12 list the seasonal factors computed with the Kuznets method.[16] These factors are simply the computed values of the regressions described earlier. The X-11 factors (columns 1 and 5) clearly dampen the changes in seasonal amplitudes. Excluding 1948 and 1949, the Kuznets factors show larger seasonal amplitudes from 1956 through 1960 than the X-11 factors and smaller amplitudes elsewhere. The differences are greatest in 1957 and, expectedly, in 1958. Whereas the X-11's July factors for these years are, respectively, 87.4 and 87.9, the corresponding Kuznets factors are 85.0 and 80.4; for December the X-11 factors are 113.9 and 113.0, respectively, for 1957 and 1958, and the corresponding Kuznets factors, 118.7 and 121.6.

The adjustment's sensitivity to abrupt changes in amplitude is not solely a question of preference. One condition for a perfect adjustment is the absence of seasonality in the adjusted data.[17] Perfection aside, the seasonality that remains in the adjusted data betrays the quality of the original adjustment. In other words, even allowing a gradually

[16] The other figures in Table 12 and curves in Chart 10 are explained below.

[17] While necessary, this condition is not sufficient. The adjusted data must also remain faithful to the original in all respects other than seasonality. The trend-cycle values, for example, are free of seasonality but do not otherwise qualify as properly adjusted values of the original series. Lacking perfection, an adjustment method should evince a convergence toward no-seasonality upon successive adjustments of the data, that is, adjustments of the adjusted data. The X-11 appears to satisfy this requirement, although the present study has not considered this issue in any detail.

TABLE 11

Summary Statistics for Kuznets' Amplitude-Ratio Method Regressions,[a] 1948–65

Year (1)	Correlation Coefficient (2)	Regression Coefficient (3)	t = value (4)	Year (5)	Correlation Coefficient (6)	Regression Coefficient (7)	t = value (8)
1948	.9346	.7106	8.3102	1957	.9495	2.4562	9.5708
1949	.8826	.4643	5.9367	1958	.9434	3.0079	8.9945
1950	.7073	.2759	3.1642	1959	.9619	2.2094	11.1281
1951	.3046	.1785	1.0114	1960	.8772	1.4544	5.7780
1952	.3935	.3350	1.3534	1961	.7420	.6177	3.5004
1953	.5977	.4930	2.3575	1962	.6668	.4048	2.8294
1954	.7859	1.0771	4.0198	1963	.7134	.2911	3.2193
1955	.9130	1.5308	7.0785	1964	.6991	.2750	3.0922
1956	.9529	1.9761	9.9303	1965	.6745	.2589	2.8890

[a]The regression form for i^{th} year is as follows: Modified SI ratios for year $i = a + b$ (constant seasonal factors) + U.

Since the mean value for both variables is 100, the constant term, a, is equal to 100 $(1-b)$.

There are twelve observations for each regression.

TABLE 12

Seasonal Factors in Treasury Bill Rates for July and December Computed with the X-11 on the Original and Seasonally Adjusted Series, and with the Kuznets Method

(per cent)

	July				December			
	Original Seasonal Factors (1)	Adjustments of Seasonal Factors (2)	Implicit Factors (3)	Kuznets Factor (4)	Original Seasonal Factors (5)	Adjustments of Seasonal Factors (6)	Implicit Factor (7)	Kuznets Factor (8)
1948	96.8	100.0	96.9	95.1	103.7	99.8	103.5	104.9
1949	97.0	970.9	97.8	96.9	103.9	99.4	103.3	103.3
1950	97.3	102.1	99.3	98.3	104.6	99.3	103.8	102.1
1951	96.9	102.9	99.8	99.0	105.5	99.1	104.5	101.4
1952	96.2	103.5	99.6	98.1	106.9	99.2	106.0	102.7
1953	94.4	103.1	97.3	97.1	108.4	99.4	107.8	103.8
1954	92.4	102.3	94.5	92.9	110.5	100.1	110.6	107)7
1955	89.8	100.7	90.5	91.0	112.2	100.9	113.2	112.0
1956	88.3	99.8	88.1	87.8	113.8	102.0	116.1	114.8
1957	87.4	99.1	86.6	85.0	113.9	102.4	116.7	118.7
1958	87.9	99.1	87.1	80.4	113.0	102.4	115.8	121.6
1959	89.0	99.0	88.2	85.0	110.5	101.4	112.1	115.2
1960	91.1	99.6	90.8	89.9	107.9	100.3	108.2	109.8
1961	93.3	100.2	93.5	95.9	105.1	99.1	104.2	104.3
1962	95.3	100.8	96.1	97.5	103.5	98.5	101.9	103.1
1963	96.7	101.3	98.0	98.2	102.7	98.3	101.0	102.2
1964	97.6	101.7	99.3	98.3	102.7	98.4	101.1	102.0
1965	98.0	101.9	99.9	98.3	102.6	98.3	100.9	101.9

NOTE: Columns 1 and 5 are the original factors computed with the X-11. Columns 2 and 6 are the factors computed for adjusting the seasonally adjusted series. Columns 3 and 7 are the implicit factors obtained with the double adjustment.

changing seasonal, the moving average of the X-11 may not be sufficiently elastic to expunge all the variation that by its own criteria (i.e., its response to a second round) are seasonal. The seasonally adjusted data will in this case retain some remnants of the seasonal pattern. The experiment with the Kuznets method suggests what these remnants will look like.

To illustrate the point this study ran the seasonally adjusted data once again through the X-11. Columns 1 and 5 of Table 12 list the factors for July and December, respectively, obtained with the original adjustment; columns 2 and 6 list the factors with the second adjustment; and columns 3 and 6 the implicit factors computed by dividing the twice-adjusted series (i.e., the series obtained by adjusting the seasonally adjusted series) into the original series. When the factor in column 2 is above 100.0, the original estimate of the July factor is too low, that is, the seasonal decline is exaggerated; the implicit factor in column 3 is in this case greater (i.e., closer to 100.0) than the original factor in column 1. Conversely, when the factor in 2 is below 100.0 the original estimate is too high (i.e., the seasonal trough underestimated) and the factor in 3 is below the factor in 1. When the factor in 6 is below 100.0, the original estimate of the seasonal peak is exaggerated and correspondingly reduced in 7; when above the original estimate it is too low and therefore increased in 7. From 1956 to 1960 the machine understated the seasonal low in July. Some, but very little, seasonal low remains in the adjusted data. In the other years, however, the machine converted the original seasonal lows in the July data to seasonal highs [18] in the adjusted data. In December the seasonal from 1954 to 1960 is understated in the original adjustment and in the remaining years overstated.

Table 13 puts the same story a little differently. In 1953 the factors computed in the second adjustment (column 2) denote, with some exceptions and with a smaller amplitude, seasonal movements in the oppositie direction from those implied in the original adjustment. In 1958 the seasonal timing implied in both columns 5 and 6 is the same, reflecting the original adjustment's failure to fully re-

[18] "High" and "low" denotes positions above and below 100.0, respectively; "peak" and "trough" denotes highest and lowest, respectively. The Kuznets experiment implies the same result for July but dates the period of understatement in 1956 instead of 1954 for December.

TABLE 13

Seasonal Factors for Selected Years Computed for Both the Original and the Seasonally Adjusted Treasury Bill Rate Series

	1953				1958				1965			
	Original (1)	Ad-justed Implicit (2)	Implicit (3)	Kuznets (4)	Original (5)	Ad-justed Implicit (6)	Implicit (7)	Kuznets (8)	Original (9)	Ad-justed Implicit (10)	Implicit (11)	Kuznets (12)
Jan.	102.1	98.9	101.0	102.3	108.9	101.6	110.6	112.3	102.3	99.7	102.0	101.1
Feb.	97.0	98.5	95.6	100.0	98.4	99.9	98.3	98.1	102.0	100.5	102.5	99.9
March	99.2	100.8	100.0	98.9	92.1	98.4	90.6	91.8	100.8	101.7	102.5	99.3
April	98.9	101.1	100.0	98.6	91.0	98.1	89.3	89.7	99.3	101.4	100.6	99.2
May	98.7	100.7	99.4	98.5	92.6	95.0	87.9	89.4	97.9	101.4	99.3	99.1
June	94.9	100.1	95.0	97.3	89.4	99.7	89.1	81.9	97.3	101.4	98.7	98.5
July	94.4	103.1	97.3	97.1	87.9	99.1	87.1	80.4	98.0	101.9	99.9	98.3
Aug.	102.9	102.2	105.2	99.9	96.2	99.7	96.0	97.8	99.8	100.7	100.1	99.9
Sept.	103.9	98.9	102.7	102.0	107.4	100.4	107.8	110.5	99.8	97.7	97.4	100.9
Oct.	101.3	99.2	100.6	102.0	110.6	101.7	112.5	110.5	100.0	97.3	97.3	100.9
Nov.	100.0	97.7	97.7	101.9	110.9	102.8	114.0	110.1	100.1	97.9	98.0	100.9
Dec.	108.4	99.4	107.8	103.8	113.0	102.4	115.8	121.6	102.6	98.3	100.9	101.9

CHART 20

Unmodified SI Ratios, Seasonal Factors, Implicit Seasonal Factors,
and Kuznets' Factors for Treasury Bill Rates

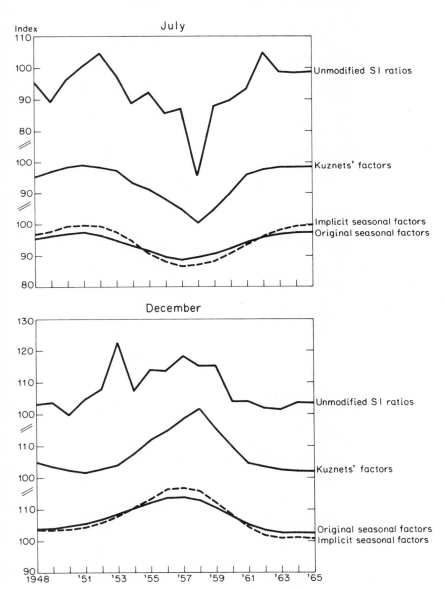

CHART 21

SI Ratios, Seasonal Factors, Kuznets' Factors, and Implicit Factors
for Treasury Bill Rates; Selected Years

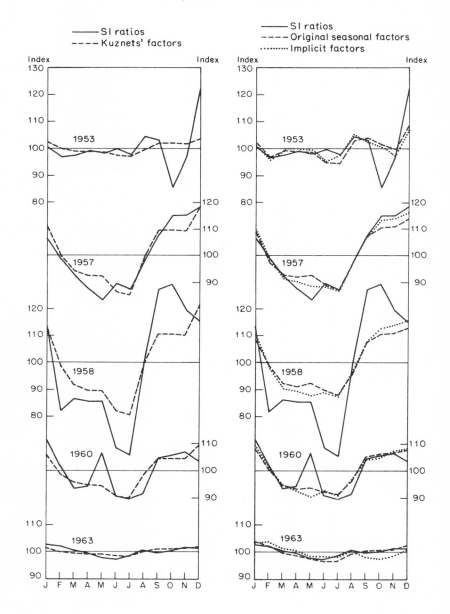

move the seasonal variance in the original series. In 1965, again the directions are reversed.

While these results confirm the expected faultiness in the machine's handling of a moving seasonal component, they emphasize even more that the magnitude of error is usually quite small; for the bill rate, with one exception, it is never more than 3 per cent of the original series and usually much less.[19] However, during the peak period the Kuznets factors differ from the original X-11 factors by up to 7 percentage points. The order of magnitude involved is shown in Chart 20 and again in Chart 21, where both the original and the implicit factors, as well as the Kuznets factors, are plotted against the SI ratios. The implicit factors appear to follow the SI ratios slightly better than do the original factors; whether they are therefore preferable is a question on which one can argue both sides. Although the double adjustment method is used in this study for illustrative purposes, further experimentation may demonstrate its usefulness as a method of adjustment when there are abrupt changes in the seasonal amplitude. Whether the single or the double adjustment is preferred there is no compelling reason to reject the machine adjustment for any part of the sample period, although some users may prefer to take the adjusted data back only to about 1953.

[19] The F-test for stable seasonality in the second adjustment indicates insignificant seasonality at any level. In adjusting the adjusted data the machine confronts the same problem of a moving seasonal and therefore likely underestimates the extent of the original maladjustment. The magnitudes involved there, however, are small, and one may safely ignore this point. In fact the opposite danger exists that the machine may confuse the relatively much greater irregular component with the seasonal one and exaggerate the extent of the original maladjustment. There is no justification, for example, for the implicit lows in September, October, and November of 1965 (column 11, Table 13).

CHAPTER 4

Determinants of Seasonal Amplitude

INTRODUCTION

THIS CHAPTER CONSIDERS some topics related to the extent and variation of seasonal amplitudes. One of the topics it deals with is the profitability of arbitrage between periods of seasonally high and low yields on long-term securities. It was found that, taking account of direct transactions and opportunity costs, a relatively small seasonal would elicit arbitrage—the more so the longer is the term to maturity, the smaller the margin requirements, and the greater the stability of the seasonal. The breakeven point for profitable arbitrage, estimated through use of hypothetical though plausible data, is below the seasonal amplitude that actually persisted through most of the study period. The result implies that a relatively high risk premium is attached to the uncertainty with which the seasonal is regarded, as well as the expected dominance of the cyclical and irregular components. The breakeven seasonal adjusted for risk would therefore be much larger. Consideration of the business and bother costs of an arbitrage operation would also raise the breakeven point.

The greater importance of term structure on short-term yield differ-

76

entials complicates the question of arbitrage in the short-term segment of the securities market. Several authors have observed that the seasonal patterns of some short-term securities lead those of shorter term securities. Since these leads are evidence of investors' awareness of the seasonal movement and more generally of their attempt to forecast short-term rates, they are also evidence of what this study is calling arbitrage. Arbitrage generally implies bridging a known discrepancy between two situations, usually between two markets at a particular time; but when the two situations occur in different periods the knowledge of the later period is at best a good forecast. The unstable character of the seasonal influence on interest rates revealed in Chapter 3 implies that using the term arbitrage in connection with seasonals is somewhat misleading. Certainly, arbitrage shades into speculation as the seasonal movement becomes more problematic.

The last section of this chapter relates changes in the seasonal amplitude of Treasury bill rates with corresponding changes in the seasonal amplitude of other series.[1] The seasonal amplitude of Treasury bill rates is inversely related to the seasonal amplitude of the stock of money and directly related to that of total bills outstanding. This finding, relevant in its own right as a description of events, serves also to illustrate the usefulness of decomposing a series to help explain its behavior. For example, when the aggregate series of interest rates and money supply are correlated, the expected inverse relation is usually obscured by the common effect of economic activity on the cyclical components of both series; although the series frequently turn at different stages of the cycle, there are many periods during which the series are moving in the same direction. However, when the cyclical component is filtered out, the expected inverse relation materializes. By replacing the original series with their seasonal factors, this study estimates the elasticity of short-term demand for credit with respect to interest rates to be a very small but statistically significant $-.0237$.[2]

[1] "Seasonal amplitude" refers to the average departure of the monthly factors from 100.0. When the pattern of factors is approximately constant from year to year the change of a given month's factor from one year to the next is a measure of the change in seasonal amplitude.

[2] The appropriateness of the concept of elasticity in the present context is evaluated in a brief appendix to this chapter.

ARBITRAGE

LONG-TERM SECURITIES

To determine the opportunity for arbitrage between seasonal phases, this study computed the effect on buying and selling prices, under a set of assumed conditions, of various seasonal amplitudes. Consider a twenty-year, 4 per cent bond with semiannual coupons whose average price over the year is the $1000 par value. Assume an investor purchases the bond at its seasonally peak yield in September and sells it, now with nineteen and one half years to maturity, the following March when yields are at their seasonal trough. The present value formula computes the prices in September and March for any desired seasonal change in yield in the following way:

$$\text{September price} = \frac{20}{(1.02 \ P.F.)} + \frac{20}{(1.02 \ P.F.)^2} + \cdots + \frac{20. + 1000}{(1.02 \ P.F.)^{40}}$$

where $P.F.$ = peak seasonal factor; e.g., 101.0; $T.F.$ = trough seasonal factor; e.g., 99.0. Semiannual coupon payment is $20; principal is $1000; and average yield is 2 per cent per half-year.

The computation leads to the result that for each one-tenth of 1 per cent in the seasonal amplitude on either side of the average value (in other words, factors equal to 100.1 and 99.9 for September and March, respectively) the price differential for a thousand dollar bond comes to approximately $10.70. For an amplitude of two-tenths of a per cent (i.e., 100.2 and 99.8) the price differential is approximately $21.40.

To estimate the seasonal amplitude necessary to encourage arbitrage this study estimated the costs and returns to this activity in two hypothetical situations: $5000 is invested with a 5 per cent and with a 25 per cent margin requirement. In the first case the investor borrows $95,000 and purchases $100,000 worth of bonds; and in the second case $15,000 and purchases $20,000 worth of bonds. Table 14 lists the estimated costs in the two situations under the following assumptions:

—Foregone interest on $5000 at annual rate of 5 per cent
—Transaction cost is $5 per $1000 bond for combined buy and sell

TABLE 14

*Costs and Returns of Arbitrage for Twenty-Year Securities Between
Seasonal Peaks and Troughs Under Certain Hypothetical Conditions*

Part A: $5000 Invested With 5 Per Cent Margin Requirement

Costs

Foregone interest[a] on $5000 for six months at assumed annual rate of 5 per cent	.025 x 5,000 =	$125.
Transactions cost (buy and sell at assumed $5 per $1000 bond	5 x 100 =	500.
Interest cost of borrowed money for six months at assumed rate of 1 percentage point above bond yield	.5 x .01 x 95,000 =	475.
Total Cost	=	$1,100.

Returns

Price differential (between September and March) at assumed $10.70 per $1000 bond for each .1 per cent of seasonal factor

$$100 \times 10.70 = \$1070.$$

Required seasonal factors to cover cost

$$100 + \frac{1100}{1070} \times .1 = 100.10\%$$

$$100 - \frac{1100}{1070} \times .1 = 99.90$$

(continued)

TABLE 14 (concluded)

Part B: $5000 Invested With 25 Per Cent Margin Requirement

Costs

Foregone interest[a] on $5000 for six months at assumed annual rate of 5 per cent	.025 x 5,000 =	$125.
Transactions cost (buy and sell) at assumed $5 per $1000 bond	5 x 20 =	100.
Interest cost of borrowed money for six months at assumed rate of 1 percentage point above bond yield	.5 x .01 x 15,000 =	75.
Total Cost	=	$300.

Returns

Price differential (between September and March) at assumed $10.70 per $1000 bond for each .1 per cent of seasonal factor	20 x 10.70 =	$214.00
Required seasonal factors to cover cost	$100 + \dfrac{300}{214} \times .1 =$	100.14
	$100 - \dfrac{300}{214} \times .1 =$	99.86

[a]The capital on which the foregone interest is computed should include half the transactions cost and approximately half the borrowing cost. The greater accuracy, however, will not significantly improve the estimates.

—Interest cost of borrowed money exceeds bond yield by 1 percentage point per year.[3]

The required peak and trough seasonal factors are computed for breakeven, account being taken of the opportunity costs of the investment.

While the estimated returns obviously depend on the conditions assumed to prevail, the orders of magnitude are established. The smaller the margin requirements, or obversely, the greater the amount borrowed relative to capital, the smaller is the seasonal amplitude required to produce the breakeven price differential. In the example, with a 5 per cent margin requirement the seasonal factors must exceed 0.10 per cent on either side of the level of rates to just cover the arbitrageur's costs. (While the example does not illustrate the point, it is also true that the greater the term to maturity, the greater the effect on the price differential of any given differential in yield.) When the margin requirements rise to 25 per cent, the required seasonal factors are 0.14 per cent on either side of the level of rates to just cover costs.

The long-term series considered in this study do not differentiate among terms to maturity; therefore, this study did not estimate the relation between term to maturity and the breakeven seasonal factors. However, one certainly expects the seasonal amplitude to diminish with an increasing term to maturity, since the longer the term the sooner will a given seasonal amplitude invite arbitrage. This point may explain the greater amplitude in three- to five-year Treasury securities than in the equivalent long-term securities and in the Treasury bill rates than in the nine- to twelve-month securities. It may also help explain the smaller amplitude of commercial paper rates, which are often six months to maturity, than in the short-term yields on bankers' acceptances and on 91-day Treasury bills.

While margin requirements vary over time and among borrowers, they are always lower for Treasury securities than for private and state-local issues. This point may account for the difference in the longevity of the seasonal amplitude in the two sets of securities, but the study makes only a *prima facie* case for the issue.

[3] The greater the difference between the long and short rate the greater is the incentive to arbitrage.

The illustrative example implies that, contrary to common opinion, there is nothing in investment behavior to preclude a seasonal influence on long-term rates provided its amplitude is sufficiently low. Since several years are required before investors perceive a seasonal, virtually any amplitude is possible for a limited period. The low breakeven points for eliciting arbitrage, 0.10 per cent and 0.14 per cent, for 5 per cent and 25 per cent margin requirements respectively, computed in the example no doubt understate the true values because of additional business costs not incorporated in the example, as well as the point, noted in the introduction, that arbitrage is in effect at one extreme—speculation is at the other—of a continuum as the certainty of the differential between two situations becomes more remote.[4]

Perhaps the greater seasonal amplitude of municipal securities is explained by the greater prominence of their irregular components. It is tempting to generalize this point—the direct relation between seasonal amplitude and relative importance of the irregular component—into an hypothesis. Other influences on these variables, combined with the fact that the seasonal and irregular components are not independently estimated,[5] would tend to obscure the relation, however. Yet we do find that the rank correlations between the ratio of the variance of the irregular component to that of the whole series (Table 4, column 1) and the seasonal amplitude as measured by the variance of the factors (Table 5) increases from the earliest to the latest years.[6] The increasing correlations imply a movement toward an equilibrium trade-off between yield and certainty of principal. In the absence of other causes of seasonal differences among long-term securities, the observed differentials in seasonal amplitude combined with the observed differences in the relative importance of the irregular component would produce a measure of the rate of trade-off between

---

[4] In this regard it would be better to replace at least in principle the seasonal factors in the illustrative example with confidence intervals or perhaps some form of certainty equivalents.

[5] In fact, the bias in the computation is toward an inverse relation, which strengthens the conclusion.

[6] For the years 1953, 1957, 1963, and 1965, the rank correlation coefficients are .30, .59, .76, and .82, respectively. These figures exclude the two long-term Treasury securities, although there was no attempt to determine how their inclusion would affect the results.

the two or, in other words, a measure of risk premium.[7] While this suggestion helps to illustrate the potential uses of time series decomposition, it suffers from the same problem this study emphasized throughout: the difficulty in distinguishing variations in seasonal amplitude from irregular movements.

SHORT-TERM SECURITIES

While the cost-return analysis of seasonal arbitrage applies equally well to short- as to long-term securities, the calculation of the cost component is complicated by the greater yield differentiation among proximate maturities at the short-end of the yield curve. Whereas the nonseasonal components of the yields on twenty- and nineteen and a half-year securities are approximately the same and therefore do not affect the arbitrage, a substantial differential between a one-month and a two-month or a nine-month and a three-month security may offset any seasonal differential. The calculated costs of arbitrage must, therefore, take account of the former differential.

The tendency for yield curves, the curves relating yield to maturity with maturity, to incline at a diminishing rate is a widely observed phenomenon and its explanation a subject of considerable dispute. Some writers attribute the phenomenon to the greater number of investors with short-term liabilities who prefer to match the maturities of their assets and liabilities than investors with long-term liabilities having similar preferences—the so-called hedging theory. Others emphasize investors' preference for short-term securities to minimize their vulnerability to capital losses—the liquidity preference theory. In either case yields increase with maturity to equilibrate supply and demand. Finally, the expectations hypothesis associates the yield structure with investors' expectations of future interest rates. While this theory does not account for the observed average incline in the yield curve, it can account for the greater differentiation among shorter term yields by recognizing the greater differentiation of investors

[7] In this context there is no need to consider differences in cyclical variation, which could further account for *aggregate* yield differentials among the various groups of securities, since the seasonal and irregular components abstract alike from the cyclical components of all the series. In principle, this measure of risk premium captures the true relation between the relative *dispersion* of yields and the yield differential of competitive securities as distinct from differences in the expected yields of the securities.

among their shorter span forecasts, for which they have more information, than their longer span forecasts, for which they are likely to rely
more on extrapolations.[8]

In evaluating the empirical basis for the expectation hypothesis,
Macaulay found evidence of market forecasting in the fact that the
seasonal peak in yields on time loans preceded the peak in call loans.[9]
Banks, he said, aware of the seasonal peak in call money rates during
December, would not tie up money in, say, November, without
insuring a return comparable to the average return on call money
during the two months. The yield on time money would therefore
peak earlier. With respect to this phenomenon, its amplitude would
have to be smaller, as well. Consider the same phenomenon from the
borrower's point of view: To avoid the December rush he can borrow
in November for two months, perhaps lend the money for one month,
and in effect acquire a forward loan for December at the lower
November rate. These transactions would have the effect Macaulay
observed, in addition to smoothing the one-month seasonal. But the
borrower's ability to avoid the peak rate depends on the nonseasonal
relation between the two-month and one-month rates in November.
If the former were much greater than the latter, both rates adjusted
for seasonality, what the borrower gains by avoiding the seasonal he
loses in the term structure differential. Since this differential is known
in November, it in part determines the extent of the seasonal arbitrage
and, therefore, of the seasonal amplitude itself. This analysis, thus,
suggests that a relation exists between the slope of the yield curve
and the seasonal amplitude.

Testing for this relation obviously requires data for different but
proximate maturities. The *Treasury Bulletin* publishes series on one-,
two-, and three-month Treasury bills, but these data record the yields
on the last trading day of the month instead of weekly averages, as
in the *Federal Reserve Bulletin's* series on 91-day Treasury bills. The

[8] There are, in addition, various eclectic theories of the term structure. The
literature on this subject has grown in recent years—much more, unfortunately,
than our knowledge. Two standard works are: David Meiselmen, *The Term
Structure of Interest Rates,* Englewood Cliffs, N.J., 1961; and Reuben Kessel,
The Cyclical Behavior of the Term Structure of Interest Rates, New York,
NBER, 1965.

[9] *Op. cit.,* p. 36. Kemmerer, *op. cit.,* p. 18, observed the same phenomenon
and had the same explanation for it.

Treasury Bulletin's series therefore have a considerably greater random component distorting the estimated seasonal patterns. This study has therefore avoided the *Treasury Bulletin* data. The data do, however, illustrate this section's argument. A direct test for the relation between the seasonal amplitude of one-month rates in December and the nonseasonal yield differential between two- and one-month rates in November is available, simply, in a regression of the SI ratios for one-month bills in December on the differential in the trend-cycle components of two- and one-month rates in November. The correlation coefficient of this regression is .56; the regression coefficient, 53.56; and its *t*-value, 2.68. In general, the variance of the SI ratios for a given year (that is, the extent of seasonal amplitude) is directly related to the slope of the yield curve.[10] The converse is also true: the unadjusted term-structure data partly reflect the seasonal pattern—which was Macaulay's point.

The point is again manifest in the nonseasonal differential between nine- to twelve-month Treasury securities and 91-day Treasury bills. The average differential in July [11] is considerably greater during the period of peak seasonality, 1955–61, than during the earlier or later periods. In the period 1948–54, the mean differential in the trend cycle values of nine- to twelve-month and 91-day Treasury securities

[10] It is obviously necessary to work with the SI ratios, preferably modified for extremes, instead of the seasonal factors themselves since the factors are designed to smooth out the effects of year-to-year changes in seasonal amplitude. In other words, to the extent the above analysis is relevant the X-11 method of seasonal adjustment is inappropriate. There is nothing sacred about the December figures. In fact, the SI ratios of all seasonally high months are positively related to the slope of the yield curve, and those of all seasonally low months negatively related. In other words, the seasonal amplitude as a whole is positively related to the slope of the yield curve. While the relation for the seasonally high months is understandable, its application to the low months is less clear. Even if the principle stated in the text applied only to the high months, the observed effect on the low months would obtain due to the effect of the high months on the trend-cycle curve. This point is considered in Chapter 2.

[11] July replaces November in this calculation because of the difference in maturities involved. Here the borrower, say the U.S. Treasury, avoids the three-month peak rate in December by borrowing for nine months in July instead of for three months in December, perhaps simultaneously purchasing a six-month security to effect the forward loan. Curiously, the point in the text is most true for July, when the combination of nine- and three-month securities is appropriate to the December peak; although, to a lesser extent it applies to all the months.

was 6 basis points; in the period 1955–61, 45 basis points; and in 1962–65, 9 basis points (all figures are for July). The figures for each year for the months June through November are given in Table 15.

As much as this analysis accurately depicts one aspect of the seasonal problem it implies still another. Typically, though not always,

TABLE 15

The Differential in the Trend-Cycle Values Between
Nine- to Twelve-Month and 91-Day Treasury Securities for
June Through November, 1948–65[a]

(in basis points)

	June	July	August	September	October	November
1948	6	10	13	14	12	11
1949	-4	12	8	6	5	4
1950	0	3	8	4	5	5
1951	24	10	10	9	10	11
1952	-1	-7	5	17	13	4
1953	11	18	23	24	42	17
1954	1	-7	-13	-12	-2	12
1955	30	14	15	11	4	13
1956	11	27	25	26	25	23
1957	13	29	38	43	31	23
1958	44	54	19	-5	2	30
1959	74	78	93	67	66	70
1960	71	62	65	51	53	55
1961	44	53	50	71	64	55
1962	25	0	16	22	19	11
1963	14	9	6	13	14	23
1964	15	16	22	23	23	22
1965	11	9	16	14	14	23

[a]The figures are trend-cycle values for nine- to twelve-month securities minus trend-cycle values for 91-day bills. The figures indicate the slope of the yield curve in the designated range independently of the seasonal and irregular movements. For the present purposes the differential in the seasonally adjusted rates (that is, including the irregular component) is a relevant alternative to the figures presented here.

the slope of the yield curve is greatest when the level of rates is low.[12] Since seasonal amplitudes should depend inversely on the slope, they should also be inversely related to the level of rates, or at least the level in relation to that of adjacent years. Chapter 3 found no such relation in the data themselves. It may be, however, that this proposition works to offset a tendency in the opposite direction: In periods of tight money, during cyclical highs, it is harder or more costly to borrow money in order to arbitrage the seasonal movement. Consideration of this point concludes this section of the study.

There are as many ways to arbitrage the seasonal influence in short-term rates as there are combinations of relevant maturities. The following discussion arbitrarily selects nine- and three-month securities and deals only with the peak-to-trough and trough-to-peak relationships; although, in principle, arbitrage is feasible between any pair of months.[13] The rule in seasonal arbitrage is simply to borrow cheaply and lend dearly; that is, borrow in July and lend in December. There are two ways to effect the transaction: Borrow and sell a nine-month security in July at high prices and cover the short sale in December at low prices. Alternatively, buy a nine-month security in December and sell it, now a three-month security, the following June. The term structure would work against the arbitraguer in the first alternative and for him in the second.[14]

[12] In the jargon of the expectations hypothesis, when current rates are below their normal or typical values they are expected to rise. Longer term lenders require a higher yield in compensation for the expected capital loss. The concept is analogous to the one underlying the Keynsian liquidity preference function. Admittedly, the figures in Table 15 do not cast a very favorable light on this hypothesis; although, most sets of term structure data support it. Reuben Kessel, *op. cit.*, argues that the very short-term part of the yield curve is dominated by liquidity premia which, he argues, are positively related to the level of rates.

[13] In this connection the smoothness of the seasonal patterns of interest rates, i.e., the absence of abrupt changes between adjacent months, is understandable. The major cost of seasonal arbitrage is borrowing cost, which is, of course, a linear function of the length of the loan. It is cheaper to arbitrage between adjacent months than across a six-month period, but the smoothness of the pattern reduces the opportunity. Whether the opportunity decreases at a faster rate than the costs as the span of the transaction decreases is determinable for any specific case.

[14] In addition, short positions are more costly to finance than long positions. The borrower must pay $\frac{1}{2}$ of 1 per cent of the value of the security (annual rate) plus the interest that accrues to the security. See *A Study of the Dealer Market for Federal Securities, op. cit.*, p. 20. Moreover, the margin require-

Given the seasonal spread, the incentive to arbitrage is determined by the cost of borrowing. In periods near cyclical peaks the incentive to purchase nine-month securities in December in order to sell them the following June is limited by the higher borrowing cost. On this ground one might expect a greater seasonal amplitude, because of the reduced arbitrage, at cyclically high rates—a consideration that is apparently offset by the one noted earlier.

Aside from the cyclical effect, however, the incentive to arbitrage is influenced by the Federal Reserve's policy toward seasonal changes in the demand for credit. The Federal Reserve's failure to meet the peak demand for credit in December would by itself produce a rise in the bill rate both directly through its own operations and indirectly through the effect on the borrowing costs of arbitrageurs. Similarly, its failure to absorb redundant credit in June and July would prevent the arbitraguers' sales (to effect their capital gain) from driving the rates up. Admittedly, the failure to contract the credit supply, or more generally to diminish its rate of increase, during June and July would increase the incentive to arbitrage. This policy combined with an easy credit policy in December would, of course, lower the level of rates; but it would not eliminate the seasonal variance. Alternatively, the attempt to keep short rates high by contracting the credit supply in July and taking no action at other times would simply diminish the incentive to arbitrage and raise the December peak. In effect, it is a tight credit policy, which affects the level of rates but not the seasonality.[15] To counter the seasonal movement in interest rates, as distinct from the level of rates, requires, therefore, a relatively easy policy in December and a relatively tight one in July. The seasonal pattern in the money supply should therefore correspond with the pattern in short-term interest rates, as in fact it does. But the seasonal amplitude in money supply (that is, the extent to which the Federal Reserve alternates the relative tightness and ease) should

ment is much greater on a short position than on a long position: about 2½ per cent compared with ½ of 1 per cent on a long position in certificates. (*Ibid.*, p. 92.) It is unlikely, therefore, that this method of arbitrage would recommend itself for smoothing seasonal differentials.

[15] In both cases the change is in the over-all level of rates but not the intra-month relations. By allowing the rates in December and July to fall by the same amount, the moving average is lowered and the December peak maintained. Chapter 2 discussed this point in a related issue.

be *inversely* related to the seasonal amplitude in short-term interest rates: The more the Federal Reserve equilibrates the supply with the demand for short-term credit, the less will interest rates vary. The final section of this report investigates this relationship.

THE EFFECT OF THE SEASONAL AMPLITUDE
OF THE MONEY SUPPLY

Chart 22 plots time series of the seasonal factors for Treasury bills and money supply, and total bills outstanding. The relative lows in June and July and the highs in the fall months are clear evidence of the Federal Reserve's policy of adjusting the supply to the seasonal changes in the demand for short-term credit.[16] The series on total bills outstanding is discussed later. However, if this policy were completely successful,[17] there would be no seasonal in interest rates. Figure 2 hypothetically depicts the situation. The demand for and supply of short-term credit in November results in a given interest rate, R_n. In December there is an increase in the demand, depicted by the outward shift in the demand curve. If the Federal Reserve did not increase the supply at all—that is, in the present context, if there were no seasonal movement in the money supply—the rate of interest would rise to R_P. At the other extreme, if the Federal Reserve had fully anticipated the rise in demand and increased the supply of money correspondingly (to S_o), the rate of interest would remain at R_N. Again, in the present context that would imply a relatively greater seasonal amplitude in the supply of money. Finally, if the Federal Reserve anticipated part but not all of the increase in demand,

---

[16] The present section considers the monthly changes in the money supply synonymous with changes in the supply of short-term credit. The appendix to this chapter deals briefly with this subject to help evaluate the findings of this section.

The supply series used in this study conforms to the narrow definition of publicly held currency and demand deposits. Since time deposits do not have a significant seasonal, the broad definition of money should yield similar results; the seasonal components of both series are very similar.

[17] The word "success" is artificially vital in the current context, since the Federal Reserve did not necessarily intend to smooth out the seasonal variance in short-term rates. The desirability of eliminating the seasonal influence on interest rate is discussed in Friedman and Schwartz, *op. ct.,* pp. 292–296.

CHART 22

Seasonal Factors for Treasury Bill Rates, Money Supply, and Total
Bills Outstanding, 1948–65

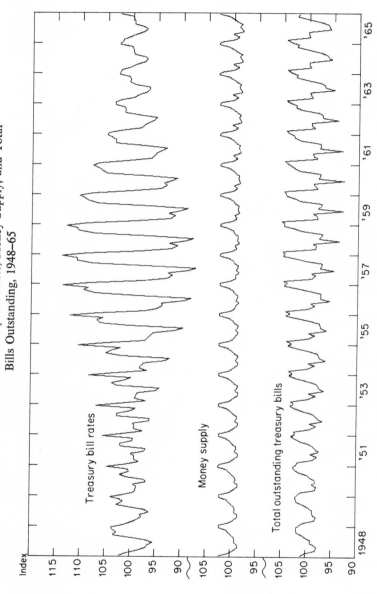

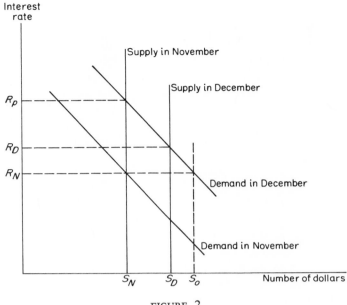

FIGURE 2

the rate would move to some intermediate position—say, R_D. The necessary seasonal amplitude in the supply of money to effect any given interest rate clearly would depend on the elasticity of demand for short-term credit: The more elastic the demand for short-term credit is with respect to the interest rate, the greater must be the seasonal amplitude in money supply necessary to prevent the seasonal increases in demand from imparting a seasonal variation to interest rates.

But how sensitive is the demand for short-term credit to the interest rate? Conversely, how sensitive is the interest rate to variations in the supply of money? Discussions of these questions typically bog down in the identification problem—that of distinguishing shifts in the demand curve from movements along it. In practice one can only observe the change in the interest rate and the change in the money supply as of a given time. Since the demand curve is itself varying, there is no sure way to associate the given readings of interest rate and money supply with a particular demand curve and, therefore, to ascertain the elasticity of the curve. The problem is soluble insofar as it is feasible to specify the variables that determine the demand curve and to fix these variables while allowing the variables affecting the supply curve [18] to move freely. In this situation, since the variables (such as income and expected changes in the price level) that determine demand are fixed, the demand curve is itself fixed, and the observed changes in interest rates and money supply may be read as points along a given demand curve. The method breaks down, however, when the same variables influence both the demand and the supply curves (such as, the preponderance of the common cyclical component in the variables affecting both curves).[19]

The study of seasonal behavior in the money market partly alleviates this problem for two reasons: (1) The use of the ratios-to-moving average of the relevant variables, or the smoothed seasonal factors, abstracts from the common cyclical component. This method is, of course, not peculiar to seasonal analysis. More importantly, (2) seasonal fluctuations in the demand for money are probably fairly stable over time; so that the seasonal shift in demand relative to the cyclical component of the shift from, say, November to December is relatively stable from year to year.[20] These seasonal

---

[18] Since the supply of new money is largely at the discretion of the Federal Reserve, to this extent the variables that affect the supply curve are those that affect the Federal Reserve's decision. This analysis presumes an autonomously determined supply of money. To the extent that the supply of money responds to interest rates apart from Federal Reserve activity, the purported separation in the determinants of supply and demand breaks down. While this point may weaken the analysis, the elasticity of supply with respect to interest rates is not likely to be sufficient to negate the substance of the analysis. In either case, the seasonal in interest rates depends on the seasonal in demand relative to supply. An endogenous supply would lessen the importance of Federal Reserve discretion in the matter of seasonality and would bias the estimated elasticity of demand for credit, since a simultaneous solution would be required. I am indebted to Walter Fisher for this point.

[19] Using averages for cyclical stages Cagan is able to show an inverse relationship between interest rates and *changes* in the money supply. (See his *Changes in the Cyclical Behavior of Interest Rates,* Occasional Paper 100, New York, NBER, 1966.) Note he relates *changes* in money supply to levels of interest rates; whereas this study deals with *seasonal* changes in both series.

[20] Since demand *per se* is not observable this proposition must be hypothesized rather than demonstrated. Some evidence in support of the proposition lies in the absence of any systematic variation in the seasonal amplitude of GNP within the study period. The implicit seasonal factors for the fourth quarter, the period of peak seasonality in the GNP, are given below. The raw

shifts are determined by economic forces outside the control of the monetary authorities. Shifts in supply, on the other hand, are subject to the discretion of the authorities. An estimate of the demand for short-term credit, therefore, is available from successive observations of the rate of interest necessary for people to hold the amount of money that is offered. More specifically, the analysis reveals the seasonal shift in the interest rate necessary for people to accept the seasonal shift in supply of money, given their *fixed* seasonal shift in demand.[21] The only fixity in this hypothetical system is in the demand for short-term credit; the interest rate varies as the supply varies—hence, the moving seasonal in interest rates.

This study's immediate purpose is not to estimate the demand for short-term credit for its own sake, but rather to investigate the causes of the changing seasonal amplitudes (i.e., from year to year) of the interest rates. Given the above analysis, the first step would be to regress the seasonal factors of Treasury bills on those of money supply, one month at a time across years. In other words, regress the January factor for bill rates on the January factor for money supply in 1948, 1949, . . . 1965: eighteen observations in each of twelve regressions. The regression coefficient, its *t*-value, and the adjusted

data, of adjusted and nonadjusted series, are given in *The National Income and Product Accounts of the United States, 1929–1965*, pp. 11 and 30.

Year	Implicit Factors Fourth Quarter	Year	Implicit Factors Fourth Quarter
1948	107.2	1957	106.0
1949	106.7	1958	105.9
1950	105.7	1959	105.9
1951	105.3	1960	105.8
1952	105.6	1961	105.8
1953	106.0	1962	105.9
1954	105.6	1963	105.8
1955	105.3	1964	105.6
1956	105.9	1965	106.6

[21] The terminology used here, admittedly awkward, does not imply that the demand is for money to hold as an asset; a demand for which there is no obvious reason for a seasonal increase in the autumn. In the present context the "demand for money" is only an abstraction that may help explain the inverse correlation between the seasonal amplitudes of money supply and Treasury bill rates. The appendix to this chapter considers this point in greater detail.

coefficient of determination are listed in Table 16. While the results are far from conclusive, in the five cases where the regression coefficients are statistically significant they reveal the expected inverse relation between the demand for money and the interest rate.

While the assumed stability in the seasonal demand for credit is plausible in the case of private demand, the government may have occasion to vary its demand both to meet changing fiscal requirements and, where possible, to take advantage of any seasonal in interest rates that may occur. Introduction of this factor, in the form of variation of total bills outstanding, leads to a considerable improvement in the estimates. The results, analogous to those in Table 16 but with the addition of total bills outstanding, are shown in Table 17. Eight instead of five of the money supply coefficients are significant,

TABLE 16

The Regression of Seasonal Factors of Treasury Bill
Rates on the Seasonal Factors of Money Supply, 1948–65

	b	t	$R^2(\text{adj})^a$
January	3.9474	.8381	v.s.
February	−9.4012	−6.3215[b]	.69622
March	1.4503	.4107	v.s.
April	−.9290	−.8665	v.s.
May	−9.2617	−2.0270[b]	.15460
June	−4.4874	−1.6004	.08412
July	14.3076	.9028	v.s.
August	.0644	.0279	v.s.
September	.6536	1.3084	.04020
October	−20.6351	−4.0472[b]	.47498
November	−23.4467	−2.0905[b]	.16545
December	−8.4171	−2.0905[b]	.16545

NOTE: Each of the twelve regressions is specified as follows: seasonal factor (bill rate) = $a + b$ [seasonal factor (money supply)]$+ E$. Each regression is run with eighteen observations.

[a]v.s. (very small) indicates that the estimated adjusted coefficients of determination are negative.

[b]Statistically significant at 5 per cent level.

TABLE 17

*Regression of Seasonal Factors of Treasury Bill Rates on
the Seasonal Factors of Money Supply and Total
Bills Outstanding, 1948–65*

	b_{MON}	t	b_{TOT}	t	R^2(adj)
January	−7.8027	−2.6531[a]	2.4944	6.8616[a]	.73768
February	−12.6356	−11.0352[a]	−.6275	−4.9796[a]	.87787
March	.1628	.0468	1.5159	1.5604	.03512
April	−7.7407	−5.6509[a]	6.7563	5.5998[a]	.64973
May	−9.9774	−1.7788	−.3225	−.2443	.10181
June	−9.0975	−4.9189[a]	1.3450	5.5671[a]	.68138
July	18.7018	1.0639	−.8688	−.6337	−.05029
August	−12.1313	−3.0136[a]	3.2720	3.3853[a]	.35756
September	.7938	1.7885	−1.2068	−2.3739[a]	.25581
October	−25.5305	−4.6300[a]	1.8186	1.7840	.53800
November	−39.3554	−4.8579[a]	10.4859	4.7151[a]	.64137
December	−2.6776	−3.1134[a]	3.8698	19.5437[a]	.96636

NOTE: Each of the twelve regressions is specified as follows: seasonal factor bill rate) = $a + b_1$ [seasonal factor (money supply)] + b_2 [seasonal factor (total bills outstanding)] + E. Each regression is run with eighteen observations.

[a]Statistically significant at 5 per cent level.

and each of the eight is negative. Eight of the coefficients of bills outstanding are positive, and six of these are significant. That is, in most, but not all, cases where the coefficients are statistically significant they have the expected sign: Increases in the money supply reduce the bill rate; while increases in bills outstanding increase the bill rate.

To obtain these results it is obviously necessary to run the regressions one month at a time across the years (or to use the equivalent dummy variable technique described below) since the month-to-month changes in the seasonal factors of Treasury bill rates and money supply have virtually the same directions and are positively correlated. During a cyclical upturn both the demand for money and the supply of money increase, but since the demand increases faster than the supply, the interest rate increases as well. In this situation, an increase in the supply of money coincides with an increase in interest rates, and the careless observer sees a positively sloped demand curve. Similarly, over the course of the year the demand for money changes in the same direction as the supply but faster, so that the interest rate varies in the same direction as the supply. However, working with deviations from the trend-cycle component isolates the common cyclical component in the demand and the supply; and estimating the relation between interest rates and money supply for one month at a time in effect exploits the relative constancy in the seasonal shifts in demand. It is then feasible to measure the points of intersection between the fixed demand curve and the varying supply curve and, therefore, to estimate the elasticity of demand with respect to the interest rate.

Instead of estimating twelve separate regressions (one for each month) of the seasonal factors for Treasury bill rates on those of the money supply and the total number of bills outstanding, it is preferable to pool all the observations and isolate the intrayear, month-to-month movements by means of dummy variables. Table 18 lists the results of this regression estimated both ways, with and without dummy variables. In regression A, without dummy variables, the common seasonal patterns dominate the relation between the seasonal factors of Treasury bill rates and money supply, and thus the regression coefficient is positive. In terms of the schematic representation, both the demand and the supply curves vary together, the demand varying more than the supply; therefore, the interest rate varies with the supply. An analogous result is frequently observed in the positive correlation between interest rates and money supply over the business cycle when no allowance is made for the joint movement of supply and demand.

In regression B, however, dummy variables for each month prevent the joint movement of supply and demand from month to month from obscuring the inverse relation between interest rates and the supply of money. The dummy variables, in effect, permit the substantive coefficients to summarize only the movement from, say, January 1956 to January 1957 and February 1951 to February 1952, instead of the movement from June 1958 to July 1958. In so doing, it allows the varying supply across all the Decembers to intersect the

TABLE 18

Multiple Regression Statistics for the Pooled Data of the Seasonal Factors of Treasury Bill Rates on Those of the Money Supply and the Total Number of Bills Outstanding, All Months, 1948–65

A Without Dummy Variables for the Months	B With Dummy Variables for the Months
b_{MON} = 1.6002 $t_{b(MON)}$ = 4.9316	b_{MON} = -3.6817 $t_{b(MON)}$ = -4.3944
b_{TOT} = .5904 $t_{b(TOT)}$ = 3.7776	b_{TOT} = 1.0767 $t_{b(TOT)}$ = 5.3460
R = .6540	R = .8471
R^2_{adj} = .4223	R^2_{adj} = .6993

NOTE: The regressions are computed with time series of the seasonal factors of the three variables: Treasury bill rates, money supply, and total bills outstanding. The first observation is January, 1948; the second, February 1948; and the thirteenth, January 1949. Regression A looks as follows:

$$\text{Factor (bill rates)} = a + b_{MON} \text{ Factor (Money)} + b_{TOT} \text{ Factor (TOTAL)} + \epsilon$$

The constant term is not shown. Regression B looks as follows:

$$\text{Factor (bill rates)} = a + b_{MON} \text{ Factor (Money)} + b_{TOT} \text{ Factor (TOTAL)} + b_i D_i + \epsilon$$

where b_i is the regression coefficient of the dummy variable for the ith month; eleven in all. These coefficients are not listed in the table.

seasonally fixed demand for December. In this way it traces out the demand curve.[22]

An alternative estimation form to depict the seasonal influences of money supply and government borrowing makes use of the variances of the seasonal factors described in Chapter 1. The variance of the monthly factors, computed for each year, measures the amplitude of the seasonal factors. Regressing the variance of Treasury bill rate

[22] The higher correlation coefficient in regression B is due to the introduction of the dummy variables. Not all of the variation of the seasonal factors of Treasury bill rates is due to the variation of the two independent variables. But since the seasonal factors for bill rates are not constant throughout the period, their average values, which are reflected in the regression coefficients attached to the dummy variables (not shown) do not explain all their variation.

TABLE 19

Multiple Regression Statistics for the Variance of the Seasonal
Factors of Treasury Bill Rates on the Variances of the Seasonal
Factors of Money Supply and Total Bills Outstanding, 1948–65

	b	t_b	Constant	Partial Correlation	R	R^2_{adj}
Money supply	−75.1311	−5.1253		−.7978		
Total bill			114.4613		.8969	.7783
Outstanding	6.7873	6.8102		.8693		

NOTE: The regressions are computed with time series of the variances of the monthly seasonal factors for each series. For a given year
and series the variance is computed of the twelve factors from January
through December. Since the mean factor is 1, a greater seasonal amplitude implies a greater dispersion around the mean and hence a
greater variance. The form of the regression is as follows:

Var. (Fact. Bill Rates) = CONST. + b_{MON} Var (Fact. Money Supply)

+ b_{TOT} Var (Fact. Bills Outstanding) + residual

factors (eighteen observations) on the variance of money supply and
total bills outstanding factors reveals the inverse and direct relationships, respectively, of the seasonal influence of these two series on
the bill rate seasonal. The results of the regression are recorded in
Table 19.

It is of course not possible to distinguish intentional changes in
the seasonal variation of government borrowing to take advantage
of the seasonal in interest rates from the unintentional responses to
seasonal fiscal requirements.[23] The Treasury's ability to adjust the
timing of its offerings to benefit from seasonal lows in interest rates
is not unlimited. It is pointless to borrow merely because the rate is
low. The problem here is analogous to the arbitrage issue discussed
earlier in this chapter.

[23] In the case of the money supply, the Federal Reserve was merely assumed
to have discretion over the supply. To the extent this assumption is unwar-
ranted the distinction discussed in the text applies to the money supply as well.
However, arguments against Federal Reserve control of the money supply
rely to a large extent on the variability of time deposits, which, in the absence
of a seasonal, are not germane to the present discussion.

TABLE 20

Multiple Regression Statistics for the Pooled Data of the Seasonal
Factors for Money Supply on Those of Treasury Bill Rates and Total
Bills Outstanding, All Months, 1948–65

b_{bill}	=	$-.0237$	$t_{b(bill)}$	=	-4.3944
b_{Tot}	=	$.0884$	$t_{b(Tot)}$	=	5.4861
R	=	$.9849^a$			
R^2_{adj}	=	$.9681^a$			

NOTE: The regression is computed as follows:

$$\text{Factor (money)} = a + b_{bill} \text{ Factor (bill rate)} + b_{Tot}$$
$$\text{Factor (Tot)} + b_i D_i + \epsilon$$

where: Factor (money) = the seasonal factors of money supply; Factor (bill rate) = the seasonal factors of Treasury bill rates; Factor (total) = the seasonal factors of total bills outstanding; and b_i = regression coefficient of dummy variable for i^{th} month.

[a] The correlation coefficient is very high because the dummy variables explain a large part of the seasonal variation of money supply. The strength of this relationship is due to the relative stability of the seasonal factors of money supply and their susceptibility, therefore, to the dummy variable technique for seasonal adjustment. (This point is considered in Chapter 2.)

From the above analysis it is a small step to compute the actual elasticity of demand for money with respect to the short-term interest rate. To do this, the variables in regression B of Table 18 have simply been rearranged.[24] Now the seasonal factors for money supply form the dependent variable, and the seasonal factors for Treasury bill rates one of the independent variables. Since these variables are already expressed as percentages of the moving average, the regression coefficients signify elasticities. The elasticity of demand for short-term credit with respect to the short-term interest rate according to this method of estimation is $-.0237$ (Table 20). The puniness of the estimated elasticity by no means implies its economic insignificance. On the contrary, it implies that a relatively small change in money

[24] The pooled data were used for this experiment since the regression coefficients computed with the variance data are further removed from the concept of elasticity.

supply will have a relatively large short-run impact on interest rates. Chart 22 foreshadowed this result in the association it showed between the relatively small changes in the seasonal amplitude of money and the relatively large changes in the opposite direction of the seasonal amplitude of Treasury bill rates.

Interpretation of this result, however, must take account of an important limitation of the estimation procedure used. By definition the seasonal factors for a given month are serially correlated, one year with the next. If the factor is high in December 1952, it will be high in December 1953 as well. This serial correlation in the observations severely limits the actual degrees of freedom as distinct from the nominal amount. In effect, the seasonal amplitude of Treasury bill rates is low, then high, then low; and that of the money stock high, then low, then high. In addition to these three points, there are smaller changes in between, especially with respect to the variation of the several months; but the total is not even near the nominal 202 degrees of freedom.[25] The uncertain degrees of freedom reduces the importance of the estimated test of significance of the estimated elasticities. The figures are therefore less reliable estimates, although there is no reason for thinking them biased. In any case, the relations described constitute an hypothesis that further work can corroborate or refute.

CONCLUSIONS

This chapter reached the following conclusions:

(1) A seasonal variation in long-term bonds can survive arbitrage so long as the amplitude does not exceed some specified amount. This amount will be greater the more important is the irregular component of the series, the shorter is the maturity of the bond, and the greater is the margin requirement for borrowing money to purchase bonds. There are, no doubt, other factors that this section did not consider.

[25] The number is computed as follows: 12 months in each of 18 years comes to 216. There are 2 independent variables, a constant term, and 11 dummy variables. $216 - 14 = 202$. Substitution of the SI ratios for the factors will not solve this problem (though it would reduce it) because the presence of seasonality implies the serial correlation of the SI ratios.

(2) The analogous computation for short-term securities is complicated by the term structure of interest rates. Other things the same, the seasonal amplitude for a given year will be greater, the greater is the slope of the yield curve. Since the yield curve is typically steepest when the level of rates is low, the seasonal amplitude on this account should be greatest when the level of rates is low. This consideration is apparently offset by the higher borrowing costs to arbitrageurs, when the level of rates is high.

(3) The variation in the seasonal amplitude of the Treasury bill rate is closely related to the movement of the seasonal amplitudes of money supply and total bills outstanding. These relationships demonstrate the influence over the seasonal in the Treasury bill rate enjoyed by the Federal Reserve and the U.S. Treasury.

(4) There is an inverse relation between the seasonal amplitude of Treasury bill rates and that of money stock. This relationship implies a negatively sloped demand curve for money with respect to interest rates. The elasticity of this curve is very small.

APPENDIX

There are at least three interpretations of what the text calls the estimated elasticity of demand for money with respect to interest rates: the slope in the observed regression of the logarithms of money supply on interest rates; the elasticity with respect to interest rates of the demand for money to hold as an asset; and the elasticity with respect to interest rates of the demand for loanable funds.

The first simply describes an observed association and is non-controversial. The second implies the interest rate is one determinant of the demand for money-as-an-asset. However, there is no reason for a seasonal in this demand; and since the method used to estimate the elasticity assumes a seasonal shift in demand, this interpretation is not appropriate. The third assumes that the only seasonally operative component of the change in the supply of loanable funds is the supply of new money so that, given the demand for loanable funds, the shift in supply due to the change in money supply would determine the interest rate. But with a lower interest rate the demand for money-as-an-asset would rise and offset—partially, totally, or more than offset, depending on the relevant elasticities—the new money component of loanable funds. Therefore, according to the third interpretation the estimate of the elasticity of demand for loanable funds is biased downward (in absolute magnitude) because the change in loanable funds is less than the change in money supply.

This problem is only one illustration of the difficulty in specifying the conditions for which a demand curve is drawn. As already noted, the method used here avoids the problem of a cyclical component common to both the supply of and demand for money. Its reference to month-to-month variation probably alleviates other difficulties encountered in demand studies.[26] Its short-term character obviates consideration of the effect of additional supplies of money combined with lower interest rates on nominal income and, through income, the increased demand for money for transactions purposes. Depending on the relevant elasticities and periods of adjustment, addition.l money could conceivably raise rather than lower the interest rate by increasing the demand for money both as an asset and as a medium of exchange. With the increased income the demand for loanable funds would rise. All these effects could offset the effect on interest rates of the increased supply of money. In addition, the short-run analysis obviates consideration of the effect of a change in interest rates on the proportion of income that is saved, which would, in turn, affect the supply of loanable funds. For the same reason any effect of the change in money supply on the price level and, through this effect, on interest rates is also outside the scope of this analysis.

These points have in common the difficulty of holding constant nominal (or real) income, fixing the demand curve for money while the supply of money is allowed to vary. Variation in money supply implies variation in income and that, in turn, implies shifts in the demand curve for money. The relationship among the three—money supply, income, and demand for money—is stronger the greater is the period allowed for adjustment. Choosing coeval observations of the relevant variables that span brief periods (months, for example, instead of years) limits the process of diffusion of the new money supply and alleviates the identification problem. To the extent, how-

[26] Some of these difficulties are noted by Milton Friedman and Anna Jacobson Schwartz in a preliminary draft of their study of monetary trends (forthcoming from the National Bureau).

ever, that the diffusion process is anticipated in the market, as, for example, when increases in money supply are taken to forebode inflation, estimated parameters based on short-period observations will suffer from the identification problem.

These problems in demand analysis are by no means peculiar to this study nor even to analyses of the demand for money, although the ubiquity of money may aggravate the problems of demand analysis. Ultimately, one is sure only of the first interpretation, namely that the estimated parameters described an observed association. Depending on how the problem is set up—how the demand curve is specified, what is the source of the observations and their time dimension—and what relationship among the variables is assumed, the writer can infer behavioral parameters from the observed association. It is then his responsibility to justify the inferences.

CHAPTER 5

Summary and Conclusions

THERE IS COMPELLING evidence of the presence of repetitive seasonal movements in both long- and short-term interest rates in the years between 1955 and 1960. Outside this period, both before and after, the evidence is less conclusive, and certainly the seasonal movements are smaller. Nevertheless, a seasonal pattern apparently existed in most of the rates studied over a period substantially longer than the brief period of peak seasonality. This result is largely predicated on the demonstrated similarities among the seasonal patterns of the several rates, as well as the relative uniformity of the pattern for a given rate over an extended period. The study's primary focus is on the quality of the evidence for these conclusions.

The seasonal factors for short-term rates are found typically to decline from a relative high in January through the spring months to a trough in June and then sharply increase to September, from which they rise gradually to a peak in December. This pattern is conspicuous in the late fifties but occurs with some variation throughout the postwar period. The amplitudes, however, vary considerably, rising gradually after the early fifties through 1957 or 1958 and falling off quite rapidly thereafter. By 1965 the seasonal movement had all but vanished, although recent evidence not considered in this study indicates some resurgence in the seasonal.

The seasonal pattern for yields on bankers' acceptance is, perhaps, the most stable of those examined, although its amplitude is somewhat less than that of Treasury bill rates. During part of the period of peak seasonality, the amplitudes, that is the variation from seasonal high to seasonal low, exceeded 20 per cent of the level of the series. These amplitudes dropped sharply after 1959. By 1963, the seasonal pattern for bankers' acceptances virtually disappeared. The seasonal pattern for Treasury bills appears to have continued through 1965, the end of the study period, although its amplitude then was barely 2 per cent of the level of the series. The seasonal movement in commercial paper rates is far less stable and its amplitude smaller than those of the other two series.

While this study did not specifically evaluate the relation between seasonal amplitude and term to maturity, there is an obvious decline in both seasonal amplitude and the period over which there is a measurable seasonal factor, as the maturity of Treasury securities increases. The patterns of the seasonal factors of long-term rates are less stable than those of the short-term rates (except commercial paper) and have a much smaller amplitude. In the early fifties the pattern typically starts with a January low that falls to a trough in March, then rises to a plateau extending from June to October, before declining to an intermediate position for the last two months. The patterns for all the private long-term bonds are alike with respect to their midyear highs and January lows, the characteristic distinguishing these patterns from those of the same securities in the later period, as well as from the patterns of the short-term rates. Starting in 1955 the seasonal patterns of private long-term bond rates change—the January factors from lows to highs and the June and July factors from highs to lows. The troughs remain in March and April and the peaks in September and October. As in the case of the short-term rates the amplitude is greatest in the late fifties and tapers off thereafter. By 1965, the amplitude is very low and in some cases nonexistent.

While this evidence strongly supports the view that seasonality exists in the interest rate series, questions relating to the methods, as well as the desirability of adjusting the data for seasonal variations remain. In addition to the sampling problem of drawing from a hypothetically stable population (a common problem of empirical economics), the estimation of seasonal factors must cope with the effects of a shifting population. That is, the seasonal factors for a given month estimated for different years differ not merely because of random fluctuations but also because the true value, apart from randomness, may itself be varying. The difficulty in empirical seasonal analysis is to distinguish the random from the systematic variation of the seasonal factors. While it is possible to devise tests of the significance of differences in estimated factors for nonoverlapping periods, a continuous reading of their accuracy from year to year is elusive. Visual comparisons of the adjusted with the nonadjusted data (or, correspondingly, the seasonal factors with the ratios-to-moving average) may help to determine whether the estimated seasonal component captures the systematic seasonal movements of the raw data. Unfortunately, this method ties the conclusions to the particular analyst and invites differences in judgment. Because of the subjectivity of this element, the study merely suggests the periods within which the factors are deemed relatively accurate.

While the similarity in the patterns of all the long-term rates considered is strong evidence of a seasonal element in the rates, the patterns themselves may not be sufficiently stable to warrant an attempt to eliminate this element. The question whether a seasonal pattern exists is distinct from the question whether the seasonal movement is sufficiently stable to justify seasonally adjusting the data and risking the introduction rather than the elimination of variation. It is often maintained that a seasonal pattern in long-term rates would not persist because of the profits available to those who would arbitrage the seasonality away by buying securities in periods of seasonally high rates and selling them when the rates are seasonally low. This argument is true only to the extent the seasonal amplitude is sufficient to cover the costs of arbitrage, including the risk that on any given occasion the cyclical, trend, or random components may swamp the seasonal effect, and to the extent the seasonal movement is sufficiently stable to make the arbitrage more than a mere speculation. The greater the importance of these two effects—swamping by other components of variation and instability from year to year—the greater will be the seasonal amplitude that will survive arbitrage. Municipal bond yields, for example, a series with a large irregular component and an unstable seasonal component, has a relatively high seasonal amplitude.

The cause of the variation in seasonal amplitudes, the salient characteristic of the seasonals observed in this study, is a complex issue. At the risk of oversimplification this study considered the problem in the light of the supply of and demand for money. On the assumption that the seasonal variation in the demand for money is relatively constant from year to year, the change from year to year in the seasonal patterns for short-term interest rates would depend on that of the seasonal patterns for the supply of money. In years when the seasonal factor for, say, January in money outstanding is high the corresponding seasonal factor for interest rates would be low; and when the former is low the latter would be high. The observed relationship between the changing seasonal factors of money supply and short period interest rates is, indeed, inverse. Hence the data are consistent with the hypothesis that the rise in the amplitude of the seasonal variations in interest rates during the 1950's and its virtual disappearance during the 1960's is attributable to changes (in the opposite direction) in the seasonal movements in money supply. This inverse relationship is more conspicuous when allowance is made for seasonal movements in the quantity of bills outstanding, a finding consistent with the hypothesis that the Treasury made some attempt to benefit from the seasonal variation in interest rates. Failure to take account of this effect, which involves a change in demand in the same direction as the change in supply, obscures the relation between money supply and interest rates. When this change in demand is statistically nullified the full effect of the change in supply is observable.

INDEX

Additive adjustment, 24–25

Amplitude, seasonal, 6, 6–10, 12–13, 28, 32, 36, 41, 43–46, 52, 56–71, 76–103, 106

Analysis of variance, 20n, 27–28, 29n

Arbitrage, 9, 76–77, 78–89, 98, 106

Bankers' acceptances, 4c, 7, 9, 10c, 30t, 36–38, 36t, 41, 47t, 64t, 81, 105

Bankers' acceptance rates, 10c, 42c, 43t

Bills outstanding, 77, 89, 90c, 94–95, 95t, 96, 97t, 98, 98t, 99t, 101

Burns, Arthur F., 17n, 19n, 26n, 67n

Business cycle, 15

Cagan, Phillip, 92n

Call loans, 84

Call money, 5c

Call money rates, 3, 4, 6n, 7

Capital markets, 7, 18

Census, U.S. Bureau of, 2
  See also X-11 seasonal adjustment program.

Commercial paper, 4c, 7, 36t, 47t

Commercial paper rates, 30t, 31, 32, 34, 39c, 41, 42c, 43t, 54, 64t, 81

Consumption, 20

Corporate bonds, 8n, 13c, 45t, 46, 47t, 48t, 50t, 51t, 58, 59c, 60c, 63c, 64t

Cost-return analysis, 83

Credit,
  demand for, 1–8, 21, 77, 91, 99, 102
  short-term, 1–2, 3–8, 8–9, 77, 89
  supply of, 1–2, 3, 7–8, 21, 88
  trade, 5, 6n

Crop movements, 3, 5, 7

Currency, 6, 18, 89n

Cyclical component, 76, 77, 83, 92, 96

Demand curve, 89–92, 96–97, 102

Demand deposits, 89n

Dummy variable, 20, 95–97, 100n

Eisenpress, Harry, 15n, 17n

Expectation hypothesis, 83, 87n

Extreme movement, 24

Extreme observations, 20

Extreme points, 32n–34n

F-statistic, 20, 29–32, 43, 54–58, 75

F-test, 30t, 44t–46t

Federal Reserve, 1, 3, 6–8, 32, 88–89, 92, 98, 101

Federal Reserve Act of 1914, 6, 23

Federal Reserve *Bulletin*, 84

Fisher, Walter, 92

Fractional reserve system, 6

Friedman, Milton, 6n, 23n, 89n, 102n

Funds,
  supply of, 5

GNP, *see* Gross National Product

Government dealer positions, 5n–6n

Government fiscal activity, 7

Government securities, 4c, 5n–6n, 7n, 8n, 11c, 22, 47t, 64t, 70t, 72t, 90c, 93
  long-term, 7n, 9–10, 11c, 31, 47t, 48t, 50t, 51t, 53c, 64t, 85, 86t
  Municipal, 4c, 8n, 9, 10c, 12c, 31, 44t, 47t, 48t, 50t, 51t, 56–58, 57c, 63c, 64t, 82, 106
  nine- to twelve-month, 7, 9–10, 31, 36t, 40c, 41, 43t, 47t, 64t, 85, 86t
  ninety-one day, 7, 84–86
  state and local, 4c, 8n, 9, 10c, 12c, 31, 44t, 47t, 48t, 50t, 51t, 56–58, 57t, 62c, 63c, 64t, 82, 106
  three- to five-year, 9–10, 43, 45t, 47t, 48t, 50t, 51t, 55c, 64t, 81

109

Date Due

DE 26 '79			

Demco 38-297